Safe School Design

A Handbook for Educational Leaders

Applying the Principles of Crime Prevention Through Environmental Design

by

Tod Schneider

Hill Walker

Jeffrey Sprague

ERIC Clearinghouse on Educational Management
College of Education
University of Oregon
2000

Safe School Design: *A Handbook for Educational Leaders Applying the Principles of Crime Prevention Through Environmental Design*

Editorial Director: Stuart C. Smith
Photographs: Tod Schneider

Library of Congress Cataloging-in-Publication Data

Schneider, Tod.
    Safe school design : a handbook for educational leaders applying the principles of crime prevention through environmental design / by Tod Schneider, Hill Walker, Jeffrey Sprague.
        p.   cm.
    Includes bibliographical references (p.   ).
    ISBN 0-86552-148-4
    1. School buildings—Design and construction—Security measures. 2. School violence—Prevention. I. Walker, Hill M. II. Sprague, Jeffrey R. (Jeffrey Richard), 1956- III. Title.
    LB3221 .S33 2000
    371.6—dc21

                                                                                        00-061694

Type: 12 pt Times New Roman
Printer: Sheridan Books, Chelsea, Michigan
UOPS: G270
Printed on recycled paper

THE ASSOCIATION
OF EDUCATIONAL
PUBLISHERS
Ed Press

FIRST EDITION
Printed in the United States of America, 2000

ERIC Clearinghouse on Educational Management
        5207 University of Oregon
        Eugene, OR 97403-5207
        Telephone: (541) 346-5044 Fax: (541) 346-2334
        World Wide Web: http://eric.uoregon.edu
ERIC/CEM Accession Number: EA 030 490

This publication was prepared in part with funding from the Office of Educational Research and Improvement, U.S. Department of Education, under contract no. OERI-RR 93002006. The opinions expressed in this report do not necessarily reflect the positions or policies of the Department of Education.

The University of Oregon is an equal opportunity, affirmative action institution committed to cultural diversity.

MISSION OF ERIC AND THE CLEARINGHOUSE

The Educational Resources Information Center (ERIC) is a national information system operated by the U.S. Department of Education. ERIC serves the educational community by disseminating research results and other resource information that can be used in developing more effective educational programs.

The ERIC Clearinghouse on Educational Management, one of several such units in the system, was established at the University of Oregon in 1966. The Clearinghouse and its companion units process research reports and journal articles for announcement in ERIC's index and abstract bulletins.

Research reports are announced in *Resources in Education* (*RIE*), available in many libraries and by subscription from the United States Government Printing Office, Washington, D.C. 20402-9371.

Most of the documents listed in *RIE* can be purchased through the ERIC Document Reproduction Service, operated by Cincinnati Bell Information Systems.

Journal articles are announced in *Current Index to Journals in Education*. *CIJE* is also available in many libraries and can be ordered from Oryx Press, 4041 North Central Avenue at Indian School, Suite 700, Phoenix, Arizona 85012. Semiannual cumulations can be ordered separately.

Besides processing documents and journal articles, the Clearinghouse prepares bibliographies, literature reviews, monographs, and other interpretive research studies on topics in its educational area.

CLEARINGHOUSE NATIONAL ADVISORY BOARD

George Babigian, Executive Director, American Education Finance Association
Anne L. Bryant, Executive Director, National School Boards Association
Vincent L. Ferrandino, National Association of Elementary School Principals
Paul Houston, Executive Director, American Association of School Administrators
Karen Seashore Louis, Vice President, Division A, American Educational Research Association
John T. MacDonald, Director, State Leadership Center, Council of Chief State School Officers
Gerald Tirozzi, Executive Director, National Association of Secondary School Principals
Michelle Young, Executive Director, University Council for Educational Administration

ADMINISTRATIVE STAFF

Philip K. Piele, Professor and Director
Stuart C. Smith, Associate Director

About the Authors

Tod Schneider is the Eugene, Oregon, Police Department's Crime Prevention Specialist and Crime Prevention Through Environmental Design (CPTED) Analyst. He also serves other law-enforcement and educational agencies through his work as a national consultant and lecturer on violence, environmental design, and confrontation management. He is an affiliate of the Institute on Violence and Destructive Behavior at the University of Oregon. Officer Schneider works closely with communities and schools in implementing violence-prevention strategies, and in creating positive school climates.

• • •

Hill Walker is codirector, along with Jeffrey Sprague, of the Institute on Violence and Destructive Behavior (IVDB) at the University of Oregon and has conducted research on students with disruptive behavior disorders in school settings for over three decades. He is a specialist in school- and preschool-based prevention and is the principal developer of the First Step to Success early intervention program for coping with antisocial behavior patterns at the point of school entry. His work in making schools safer and violence free has been broadly recognized nationally.

• • •

Jeffrey Sprague is an expert in school safety, violence prevention, delinquency, and evaluation of programs in delinquency prevention and school safety. He serves as codirector of the IVDB and is the principal investigator of the Peaceable Educational Practices Program for creating positive, safe, and effective schools. Dr. Sprague is a national expert in the above areas and is highly influential in state and federal policy initiatives in school safety and prevention of youth violence.

Preface

This resource guide was written to help school board members and school leaders create safer schools through effective design, usage, and supervision strategies. The guide is based on principles and concepts of Crime Prevention Through Environmental Design (CPTED).

The guide is a product of the Institute on Violence and Destructive Behavior (IVDB), which is codirected by Jeffrey Sprague, Ph.D., and Hill Walker, Ph.D. The institute was founded in 1994 to systematically address issues of youth violence and destructive behavior, particularly within school settings but also in community contexts. The institute is one of four centers and institutes in the College of Education at the University of Oregon that collectively house and coordinate all research, development, and outreach activities of college faculty and staff.

The IVDB's mission is to "empower schools and social service agencies to address violence and destructive behavior at the point of school entry and beyond, in order to ensure safety and facilitate the academic achievement and healthy social development of children and youth." This mission is accomplished by and through the following means:

1. conducting original research

2. developing tools and intervention programs that will address the needs of at-risk youth, their family members, and the professionals who serve them in a range of school and agency contexts

3. providing training and technical assistance to personnel, agencies, and legislative bodies in order to make schools safer, effective, and violence free

4. contributing to the development of policies and practices that will allow the best information to be accessed and applied in addressing the critical issues of school safety and violence prevention-intervention

The content of this volume focuses on this latter strategy for enhancing school safety.

This document was developed by IVDB-affiliated personnel with the goal of creating safer schools by providing school administrators and school board members with access to the extensive body of knowledge on innovations in the architectural design, use, and supervision of space in our schools.

The senior author, Tod Schneider, a crime-prevention specialist for the Eugene, Oregon, police department, has considerable expertise in evaluating and providing technical assistance to schools and community agencies in Crime Prevention Through Environmental Design (CPTED). A great deal is currently known about enhancing school safety through this avenue, but this knowledge has not been systematically applied in our public school systems.

The purpose of this book is to synthesize, integrate, and make available to school personnel solid information on this topic in the hope that it will make their tasks easier in ensuring the safety of students in the school setting as well as in the neighborhoods and communities that schools serve.

Table of Contents

List of Tables

List of Figures

List of Sidebars

List of Forms
and Other Instruments

CHAPTER
1

Introduction

The Changed Landscape
of School Safety and Security

In the decade of the nineties, the landscape of school safety and youth violence in U.S. schools changed dramatically—perhaps in ways that most observers of the educational scene could hardly have imagined. The place names of Jonesboro, Arkansas; West Paducah, Kentucky; Edinboro, Pennsylvania; Springfield, Oregon; and Littleton, Colorado, are forever etched in our collective memory.

These terrible school tragedies signaled the advent of a new and deadly escalation of violence: multiple homicides and extensive injuries of many students and adults. Since 1993, 48 students have been killed and 91 injured in school shootings (Ribbon of Promise, 2000).

Until the 1990s, most school deaths represented single occurrences; the tragedies at the above sites marked unfortunate exceptions to this pattern. For example, the U.S. Centers for Disease Control, which monitor school shootings, report that during the 1992-93 school year, there were two campus tragedies involving multiple homicides; in the 1997-98 school year, there were five. There was none in 1993-94, one in 1994-95, and four each in 1995-96 and 1996-97. These disturbing statistics reflect an ominous trend that we all hope will not continue.

On February 29, 2000, a seven-year-old boy from a dysfunctional, chaotic family background in Flint, Michigan, brought a stolen, 32-caliber handgun to school and shot to death a six-year-old girl with whom he'd had an argument the day before. This event marks yet another change in the school-shootings landscape in that both the victim and victimizer were first-graders.

That the scourge of school shootings could extend downward to this age level borders on the unbelievable—but it has. As a society, we need to understand the real risks that impinge upon children's lives in today's society, and take positive steps to prevent similar events from occurring in the future.

The public response to the spate of school shootings and myriad threats of violence from students over the past seven years has been immediate and strong, resulting in enormous pressures on school administrators to do everything in their power to make schools safer and violence free.

To date, the educational community seems to have invested primarily in a two-pronged response.

The first strategy has been to intensify conventional school-security measures, which range from I.D. cards to metal detectors. The effectiveness and appropriateness of metal detectors in the school setting con-

These students are writing appreciative comments on each others' paper capes. A positive school climate is a strong protective factor.

tinue to be hotly debated. In a further effort to enhance security, many schools have also increased the presence of school resource officers.

A second strategy has involved attempts at profiling and identifying students who may have a higher than normal risk of committing violent acts. Numerous checklists of symptoms and supposed indicators of potential violence have emerged, but little attention has been paid to their validity, which is extremely limited for the purpose of identifying, before the fact, students likely to perpetrate acts of school violence.

Profiling strategies, long used by the FBI in the search for patterns of criminal behavior, have a substantial downside risk when applied to the complex task of detecting potentially violent offenders in schools. School-based profiling is far more likely to stigmatize vulnerable youth and ruin their reputations than it is to aid in the early detection or interdiction of a potentially violent student.

This overall approach of relying on security measures and profiling techniques is fraught with limitations, and it may be appropriate only within chaotic schools that serve crime-ridden neighborhoods in some of our nation's inner cities. The majority of schools will be better served by implement-

ing alternative techniques of a more positive, enduring nature that shape the design, structure, operation, and climate of the school. We recommend that school officials consider these alternatives before resorting to the severe measures of increasing security and profiling

Characteristics of Safe and Unsafe Schools

So just how safe are today's schools? They're not as safe as we like to think. Confidential self-reports of victimization by affected youth do not confirm one of our most cherished beliefs: that schools are among the safest places for children and youth.

Dr. Paul Kingery, executive director of the Hamilton-Fish National Institute on School and Community Violence at George Washington University, reports that most young children "are at higher risk for violence *at school* than elsewhere" (Kingery, February 29, 2000).

The Hamilton-Fish Institute analyzed data from the National Crime Victimization Survey of youth conducted over a three-year period (1993-95). The results showed that 12-year-olds face higher risk of victimization by violent crime in school than anywhere else. This is particularly true for girls, who are at risk of being assaulted by both strangers and by acquaintances. Only beyond the age of 12 does the risk of victimization outside of school surpass the risk in school.

According to the survey results, 61 percent of girls and 47 percent of boys who were victims of violence by a stranger were injured in a school building or on school grounds. Of all the acts of violence perpetrated by acquaintances against 12-year-old boys and girls, 61 percent of the boys and 64 percent of the girls were victimized at school.

These results send an important message to educators, parents, and the larger society: We need to make schools safer than they currently are. School shootings garner the lion's share of media attention; it is clear, however, that a significant proportion of our children and youth are quietly victimized by the violent actions of others that do not involve lethal outcomes.

Figure 1-1 characterizes safe versus unsafe schools and lists the attributes that move schools in the direction of greater versus lesser safety. As a general rule, the research indicates safer schools tend to be ones that

• are well led

• have positive climates and atmospheres

• are inclusive of all students

• are academically effective

Schools in some states are now required to have a school-safety and/or a crisis-response plan in place. Just as many schools have a school-improvement plan, every school should have on file a comprehensive plan that addresses risk factors in regard to school safety and that prescribes procedures to follow in case of an emergency.

Figure 1-2 displays the components that are relevant to developing a school-safety plan. The more at risk the school and the more palpable the threats to its safety and security, the greater the number of these options planners should consider in constructing the overall plan.

Sources of Vulnerability to School Safety

Schools encounter vulnerabilities to their safety and security in four major areas:

1. the design, supervision, and use of school space

2. the administrative operations and practices of the school

3. the neighborhoods and surrounding communities served by the school

4. the behavioral characteristics and histories of the students who are enrolled in the school (see Sprague and Walker in press; Walker and Walker 2000).

Figure 1-3 illustrates these four areas and lists indicators under each. Typically, in the search for school-safety solutions, educators' attention is focused primarily on student backgrounds, characteristics, attitudes, and behavior patterns. However, the remaining three sources of vulnerability shown in the figure also account for significant variations in the relative safety of schools.

Ensuring the safety and security of students and staff members in today's schools is a very daunting task that requires a comprehensive approach. Our society's myriad social problems (abuse, neglect, fragmentation, rage, and so forth) are spilling over into the schooling process at an alarming rate. It is essential that school officials address these four areas systematically and identify and ameliorate the risk factors within them so that, to the extent possible, violence can be prevented and schools made safer.

The Role of Physical Design and Technology in Creating Safer Schools

Perhaps the most neglected of the four sources of vulnerability displayed in figure 1-3 is the architectural design of the school building and surrounding grounds. Safety and security were not of paramount concern when the vast majority of the nation's school facilities were designed. If school planners paid relatively less attention to this area in the past, it was because safety was lower on the list of priorities, not because planners did not know how to design safe physical plants.

Figure 1-1

Bipolar Dimensions and Attributes of Unsafe and Safe Schools with Associated Risk and Protective Factors

Unsafe Schools

(Lack of cohesion, chaotic, stressful, disorganized, poorly structured, ineffective, high risk, gang activity, violent incidents, unclear behavioral and academic expectations)

Safe Schools

(Effective, accepting, freedom from potential physical and psychological harm, absence of violence, nurturing, caring, protective)

School-Based Risk Factors

- Poor design and use of school space
- Overcrowding
- Lack of caring but firm disciplinary procedures
- Insensitivity and poor accommodation to multicultural factors
- Student alienation
- Rejection of at-risk students by teachers and peers
- Anger and resentment at school routines and demands for conformity
- Poor supervision

School-Based Protective Factors

- Positive school climate and atmosphere
- Clear and high performance expectations for all students
- Inclusionary values and practices throughout the school
- Strong student bonding to the school environment and the schooling process
- High levels of student participation and parent involvement in schooling
- Provision of opportunities for skill acquisition and social development
- Schoolwide conflict-resolution strategies

Figure 1-2

Major Components of a Prototype Safe-Schools Plan

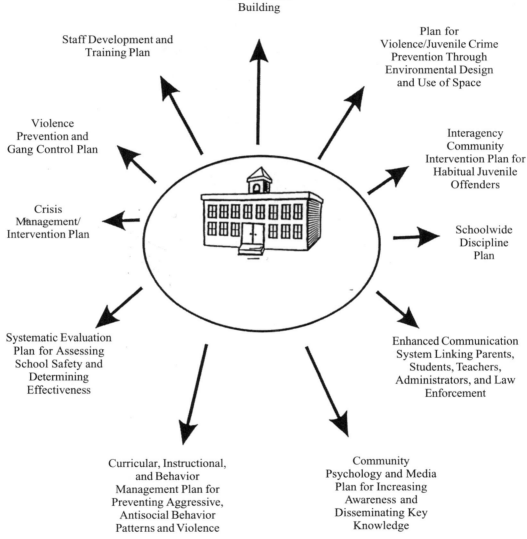

Plan for Securing the Physical Safety of the School Building

Staff Development and Training Plan

Plan for Violence/Juvenile Crime Prevention Through Environmental Design and Use of Space

Violence Prevention and Gang Control Plan

Interagency Community Intervention Plan for Habitual Juvenile Offenders

Crisis Management/ Intervention Plan

Schoolwide Discipline Plan

Systematic Evaluation Plan for Assessing School Safety and Determining Effectiveness

Enhanced Communication System Linking Parents, Students, Teachers, Administrators, and Law Enforcement

Curricular, Instructional, and Behavior Management Plan for Preventing Aggressive, Antisocial Behavior Patterns and Violence

Community Psychology and Media Plan for Increasing Awareness and Disseminating Key Knowledge

Figure 1- 3

School Safety:
Sources of Vulnerability in School Settings

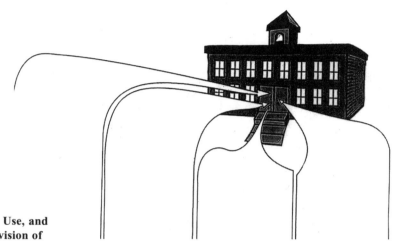

Design, Use, and Supervision of School Space

- Height of windows

- Number and type of entrances/exits

- Location and design of bathrooms

- Patterns of supervision

- Traffic patterns and their management

- Lighting

- Ratio of supervising adults to students

Administrative and Management Practices of the School

- Effectiveness and quality of administrative leadership

- Consistent, firm, and caring disciplinary procedures

- Positive, inclusive school climate

- Effective communication with students, families, and teachers

- Effective staff training and support

- Full student engagement with school processes and activities

Nature of the Neighborhood Served by the School

- Disorganization or decay

- Crime levels

- Availability of alcohol, tobacco, and other drugs

- Exposure to violent media

- Lack of afterschool activities

Characteristics of Students Enrolled

- Poverty of students and families

- Proportion of at-risk students enrolled

- Frequency and type of arrests in school and community

- School discipline referrals

- Academic achievement levels

Positive roles for older students, such as crossing guards, help to create a positive environment.

Today, planners can make use of time-tested principles of architecture to enhance safety and improve security in the design and retrofitting of schools, and they can employ newer technologies to monitor spaces and the individuals who inhabit them. These design and monitoring techniques represent highly cost-effective approaches to making school sites safer and violence free. The goals of these procedures are to prevent interpersonal conflict; to reduce the opportunities for vandalism, violence, and victimization of others; and to facilitate the smooth operation of the school building.

Social Ecology and Safe School Environments

A multitude of influences that have a bearing on school safety and security can be subsumed under the broad framework of social ecology (Moos and Insel 1974; Romer and Heller 1983; Schalock 1989). *Social ecology* refers to the complex relationships that exist between an individual's actions and the context(s) in which they occur. Social ecologists seek to answer this question: To what extent is human behavior influenced by the host of environmental factors (social and physical) that are present at any given time, and in any setting, in which the behavior occurs? Research on the antecedents of human behavior indicate that contextual factors are extremely influential in accounting for behavioral outcomes.

The field of social ecology generally focuses on two major sources of variability or influence on human actions: *behavioral* and *physical. Behavioral ecology* refers to the social contingencies, expectations, and demands that influence behavior in specific contexts and situations (for example, academic failure, bullying, and harassment).

Physical ecology, in contrast, refers to the manner in which the physical characteristics of the setting influence human behavior (for example, overcrowded classrooms, chaotic neighborhood surrounding the school, deteriorating buildings).

The behavioral ecology of the school might be reflected in rules of conduct: fighting is not acceptable and will lead to a suspension; skateboarding is against the rules. The physical ecology of the school would be reflected in its design (for example, if you fight you are very likely to be seen and caught; the texture of the sidewalk is not conducive to skateboarding).

Social ecology provides a number of important tools and principles for use in creating schools that are positive, safer, and more effective. For example, a central principle of social ecology is the concept of *person-environment fit* or match (see Schalock and Jensen 1986). School planners and architects would find it quite helpful to know how well, say, the average 12-year-old's characteristics (attitudes, skills, performance) match up or "fit" with the demands and expectations of a particular setting, such as a classroom, hallway, or soccer field.

Safe schools tend to be accommodating and supportive of the broad range of students whom they serve; safe schools are inclusive; and safe schools are also engaging

Use of Security Measures by Schools

A 1997 Public School Survey conducted by Westat for the National Center for Education Statistics asked schools which of seven security measures they used:

1. Visitors required to sign in.

2. Access to school grounds controlled.

3. Access to school building controlled.

4. School campus closed for most students during lunch.

5. Students required to pass through metal detectors daily.

6. Random metal detector checks performed.

7. Schools conducted drug sweeps.

They sorted responses into the following categories:

Stringent Security Options	2%	Full-time guard and daily or random metal-detector checks
Moderate Security Measures	11%	Full-time guard, or part-time guard with restricted access to the school, or metal detectors with no guard
Low-level Security Measures	84%	Restricted access to the school but no guards or metal detectors
No Security Measures	3%	

The survey did not directly address CPTED measures incorporated into architectural design, nor did it address the role of police in the schools.

A 1996 study by the Center on Juvenile and Criminal Justice/National Center on Institutions and Alternatives, *An Analysis of Juvenile Homicides: Where They Occur and the Effectiveness of Adult Court Intervention*, found that six states contained 56 percent of all juvenile arrests in the U.S. (Florida, Michigan, New York, Illinois, Texas, and California), and that four cities that contain just 5.3 percent of the U.S. juvenile population accounted for 30 percent of the country's juvenile homicide arrests.

of students' needs, interests, and special requirements. As a rule, schools with positive school climates tend to maximize the principle of person-environment fit for all students.

The physical ecology of the school is likewise a powerful factor in contributing to its safety, security, and effectiveness. The design and use of school space has a huge but often unrecognized impact on the behavior of students as well as staff. Overcrowded schools and classrooms and hallways that are too narrow to accommodate the number of students moving through them, for example, are likely to produce far more conflicts than less crowded physical spaces. The use of lighting, color, and building-design features can all influence how individuals feel and act in the school setting.

The Knowledge Base on Crime Prevention Through Environmental Design (CPTED)

An important knowledge base relating to the influence of the social and physical environment on safety and security has emerged over the past four decades. This knowledge has been organized and formulated into a set of principles known as Crime Prevention Through Environmental Design (CPTED).

Based on principles of social ecology, with an emphasis on physical ecology, CPTED helps us to understand how the constructed physical environment affects human behavior, and thus how it can be used to improve the management and use of physical spaces. CPTED has been used extensively in the prevention and deterrence of criminal behavior in a range of community settings, including schools. CPTED asserts that the proper design and use of the built environment can produce three important outcomes:

- reduction in the incidence and fear of crime

- improvements in quality of life

- productive use of space (Crowe 1990)

It is most unfortunate that, in the current press to create safer schools and reduce the likelihood of student violence, CPTED concepts and principles, which would be greatly beneficial to these tasks, are remarkably ignored and underutilized. We believe the CPTED approach is one of the most effective tools currently available for accomplishing these goals. The purpose of this book is to illustrate how the CPTED knowledge base can be applied productively in the effort to create safer schools.

The remaining chapters describe a full range of CPTED topics, with the goal of enabling educators and other specialists to apply these techniques successfully. Chapter 2 examines the relevance and usefulness of CPTED as a strategy for addressing school safety and security issues. Chapter 3 provides an introduction to key CPTED concepts, basic principles, guidelines, and effective application to school settings.

Chapter 4 describes site-based evaluation procedures for conducting a school safety assessment. This chapter also presents a series of recommendations for improving a school's safety and security based on CPTED assessments.

Chapter 5 takes the reader through two CPTED school-safety assessments, highlighting typical problems and recommending solutions based upon the results.

Finally, a list of recommended resources on school safety is provided in the Appendix.

A Brief History of CPTED

The roots of modern CPTED can be found in Jane Jacobs' seminal book, *The Life and Death of Great American Cities* (Jacobs 1960). In studying the impact of urban design, Jacobs found that how people take ownership of an area can have a major impact on the levels of disorder and unrest in those locations. She called upon developers, planners, and communities to build diverse neighborhoods with better opportunities for social interaction.

The term "Crime Prevention Through Environmental Design" (CPTED) first appeared in 1971 with the publication of a book by the same title, authored by C. Ray Jeffery, a professor at Florida State University's School of Criminology. Jeffery's work focused on the science of ecology and called for interdisciplinary study of "the ecology of crime" (Jeffery 1971, 1999).

Oscar Newman's *Defensible Space* followed a year later, emphasizing territoriality, surveillance, image, and "mileu"—safe zones (Newman 1972). Today, this latter concept has been renamed the "broken windows" theory. Newman's ideas were widely adopted by government and corporate groups for further development and application, with a focus on surveillance, access control, and territoriality.

During a decade of decline in U.S. applications, Canada continued to see significant strides in the application of CPTED by academicians Pat and Paul Brantingham, and by Canada's first CPTED consultants, Greg Saville and Paul Wong, all based in Vancouver. In the U.K., CPTED led to the evolution of a whole new approach called "situational crime prevention" by criminologists Patricia Mayhew and Ronald Clark.

The 1990s saw a burst of activity in the application of CPTED principles. Timothy D. Crowe brought renewed attention to the field with his 1991 book *Crime Prevention Through Environmental Design: Applications of Architectural Design and Space Management Concepts*. Crowe is personally responsible for teaching and mentoring a significant number of today's CPTED specialists, often through the National Crime Prevention Institute at the University of Louisville.

Substantial contributions to the field in recent years have also been made by the city planner and police captain team of Stan and Sherry Carter, with their successful work on the North Tamiami trail in Sarasota, Florida (Plaster 1993). Concepts dealing with the fear of crime and the role of women in public spaces were brought to CPTED by the Toronto-based women's advocacy group METRAC, based largely on the contributions of Gerda R. Wekerle. Professor Wekerle serves on the Faculty of Environmental Studies at York University, and has been influential within the Toronto Safe City committee (Wekerle 1992, Wekerle and Whitzman 1995).

Dozens of CPTED analysts have been instrumental in the field's continued evolution and dynamism, such as urban planner and criminologist Gregory Saville and Virginia Tech University Professor Diane Zahm. Others, such as Toronto high school principal Gerry Cleveland and Tucson psychologist Dennis Embry, have made important contributions to the affective side of the CPTED field, focusing on the social ecology of schools.

This dramatic growth culminated in the formation of the International CPTED Association (ICA) in 1996, in Calgary, Alberta, Canada. The ICA has grown to over 400 members in 35 countries around the world; has annual conferences, newsletters, and websites; and is in the process of establishing global professional standards for the CPTED movement. It has also taken on the task of advancing the theory and practice of CPTED beyond physical strategies, with an emphasis on the rebuilding of community.

2

The Relevance of CPTED as a Strategy for Improving School Safety and Security

The concepts and principles of Crime Prevention Through Environmental Design (CPTED) have been applied successfully in a broad range of settings and situations in the U.S. and internationally. To illustrate that diversity, here are some examples of CPTED applications in nonschool settings:

• The following cities and communities all experienced substantial reductions in crime rates by instituting CPTED measures: Atlanta, Georgia; Richmond, Virginia; Toronto, Ontario; Sarasota, Florida; the Clason Point row houses in the Bronx; Potomac Gardens in Washington, D.C.; and the Five Oaks neighborhood in Dayton, Ohio.

These communities instituted such strategies as improving control of access (for example, blocking off some streets to vehicle traffic to discourage drug dealers), defining border areas with fencing to reinforce a sense of territoriality, and improving lighting to enhance natural surveillance.

• Multistory parking garages, commonly cited as locations that generate fear and allow victimization, can be greatly improved with CPTED measures. The University of Louisville made one downtown garage safer by increasing ceiling height and lighting while also installing numerous security devices and improving natural surveillance.

A public garage in San Francisco, designed by Gordon Chong and Associates, has a sophisticated, computerized lighting scheme to illuminate all areas of the garage. Chong sought to compensate for the human

eye's difficulty in adjusting to contrasting lighting conditions. The interior of the garage is more brightly illuminated during the day so the eye can better adapt to the shift from natural outdoor light. After dark, interior lighting is subdued to more closely match the level of lighting on the streets. These arrangements allow individuals to shift between environments without temporarily compromising their ability to see while their eyes adjust to dramatically different light levels.

• Consultant Toni Sachs Pfeiffer was hired by the German National Railways to study the operation of their main railway stations. She found architectural columns that blocked views and larger fields of vision. Some visitors, unfamiliar with the space, easily became disoriented. Her architectural redesign of the space opened up viewing areas and reduced disorientation, with an accompanying increase in legitimate uses of the site. A drop in littering rates was also attributed to the redesign.

• A number of communities in Canada, Britain, France, Australia, New Zealand, and the United States have developed CPTED guidelines for use by private builders as well as by government planners. The CPTED approach has been found applicable for everything from city parks to multiunit housing complexes.

More recently, CPTED has been applied successfully to school design and retrofitting efforts throughout the United States. For example, San Diego, California, schools darkened their campuses and installed strategic fencing, and the result was a dramatic drop in campus crime rates. Darkened campuses at night make it difficult for intruders to gain undetected access to the school grounds or building. If they do intrude, use of motion-detection lights alerts others to their presence and makes them easier to detect. In addition, there is a savings on electric bills.

Equipment stored adjacent to this low roof provides easy roof access, inviting trouble.

Florida has adopted statewide school-based CPTED standards. CPTED has become a standard component of the training that school professionals receive through the National School Safety Center, affiliated with Pepperdine University, and the National Crime Prevention Institute in Louisville, Kentucky. In addition, private consultants and groups such as the International CPTED Association promote school applications of CPTED throughout the world.

CPTED as a Tool for Enhancing School Safety

Security plans for schools must be individually crafted and tailored to the needs and characteristics of specific school sites if they are to be effective. Each school represents a unique mix of histories, cultures, attitudes and expectations, physical and social realities, risk and protective factors, and resources. The incidence of crime, the risk of crime, and the fear of crime are unique to

each school and community. The physical retrofitting of an existing school site to improve its relative safety requires different considerations than does building a new school. Urban schools face different challenges than do rural ones in this regard.

Preoccupation with indoor school safety can lead school authorities to overlook exterior locations where violence is just as likely or even more likely to occur. One study found that two out of three school-based violent deaths occurred outdoors (in parking lots, on private property, on the streets, or in neighborhoods en route to or from school) (see Kachur, Stennies, and Powell 1996).

The public pressures resulting from a school tragedy can easily force administrators into considering highly visible school-security measures, such as the use of metal detectors, surveillance cameras, ID cards, or security guards. While these relatively quick and easy-to-implement strategies may be politically understandable and do improve school security to some degree, they may not be the best solutions over the long term.

In most cases, school districts' security needs will be better served by more deliberate planning and consideration of structural changes that focus on reducing risk factors and enhancing protective factors. CPTED concepts, principles, and tools can make very important contributions in this process.

CPTED Profiles of Recent School Tragedies

School-based tragedies involving student and/or staff deaths have taken place in a variety of locations. The perpetrators' motives have likewise varied. Upon close inspection, each of these acts of violence would have required distinctly different preventive measures.

Locations

Survey data on school-related violent incidents over a two-year period (1992-94), reported in the *Journal of the American Medical Association* (1996), reveal the following pattern:

- Roughly one-third of the incidents occurred inside schools (29.5 percent).
- Another one-third occurred on campus, outdoors (35.3 percent).
- The remaining one-third occurred off the school site (35.2 percent).

A review, by the senior author, of 216 National School Safety Center files on school-associated violent deaths between 1992 and 1998, in which locations were specified, documented the following:

- Indoor, on-campus deaths—76 (35 percent)
- Outdoor, on-campus deaths—97 (45 percent)
- Outdoor, off-campus deaths—41 (19 percent)
- Indoor, off-campus deaths—2 (1 percent)

The most common on-campus locations documented in the NSSC files were:

- Parking lots and school bus stops—38 percent

- Hallways and stairwells—30 percent
- Playgrounds, ball fields, school yards, or grounds—23 percent
- Classrooms, staff rooms, or school offices—21 percent
- Front steps or entry area—11 percent
- Breezeways, center courts, or quadrangles—9 percent
- Bathrooms—6 percent
- Cafeterias—5 percent

Motives

According to the *JAMA* study, motives for school tragedies are often complex in nature. The largest proportion of cases involved interpersonal, non-romance-related disputes (33.3 percent); gang-related activities (31.4 percent) were next most frequent. The remaining incidents were attributed to a range of motives including suicide (18.1 percent), romance-related disputes (11.4 percent), robbery or attempted robbery (9.5 percent), disputes over money or property (6.7 percent), drug-related activities (5.7 percent), and unintentional killings (4.8 percent).

To further illustrate the range and diversity of contemporary situations involving school violence, we have assembled in table 2-1 a variety of data on recent incidents involving multiple fatalities on school grounds. The table gives each incident's location, access paths, ages of perpetrators, and other details.

The diversity of circumstances documented in table 2-1 illustrates the need for individually tailored strategies for responding to and preventing such situations. Table 2-2 provides expert coding of these same incidents according to strategies and interventions that have varying degrees of effectiveness. Coding assigns a higher numeric value to approaches most likely to

Table 2-1

Profiles of Recent School Violence Incidents

Incident	On campus	Indoors or Out	Access path	Age	Time of day/ Details
February 29, 2000. Mount Morris Township, MI. A first-grader pulled out a gun and shot 6-year-old Kayla Rolland.	X	I	Hallway	7	Easy gun access at home; child hid gun in his clothing.
May 20, 1999. Conyers, GA. Gunman opened fire in the common area of Heritage High School, near cafeteria.	X	I	Hallway	unk	The school has a campus policeman and surveillance cameras.
April 28, 1999. Taber, Canada. A 14-year-old boy threatened a teacher and shot two students.	X	I	Hallway	14	Described as an unpopular former student, ridiculed in the past, armed with a sawed off .22 caliber rifle.
April 20, 1999. Littleton, CO. Columbine High School.	X	I	Main entry; hallways	17	Dylan Klebold and Eric Harris kill 15 with multiple guns and bombs.
May 21, 1998. Springfield, OR. Shooting. Kip Kinkel. Parked blocks away, walked in with a 22 caliber rifle and 2 handguns.	X	I	Service driveway, to breezeway, to cafeteria	15	Before school; Allegedly shot parents night before at home.
May 21, 1998. St. Charles, MO. Three 6th-grade boys' plan for a sniper attack during a false alarm was thwarted, intended as a copycat of Jonesboro, planned for June 6, the last day of school.		O	Unknown	11	Attack wasn't carried out because the boys couldn't get guns. They had recently threatened classmates.
May 21, 1998. Onalaska, WA. Suspect took girlfriend off school bus at gunpoint, took her home, shot himself.		I	Bus, foot, home	15	Suicide.
May 19, 1998. Fayetteville, TN. Honor student opens fire, kills classmate dating his girlfriend.	X	O	In parking lot	18	3 days before graduation; jealousy.
April 28, 1998. Pomona, CA. Three shot while playing basketball at elementary school after hours.	X	O	Outdoor basketball court	14	After school; group rivalry.
April 26, 1998. Edinboro, PA. One killed, 3 wounded, at school dance off campus; then walked inside club, fired more, then left.		O&I	Patio outside banquet hall	14	Loner who never smiled; .25 cal. handgun.
April 24, 1998. Jonesboro, AR. Fifteen shot, false fire alarm.	X	O	Sniped from woods	11 13	During school; fire alarm as lure.
December 1, 1997. West Paducah, KY. Heath HS. Eight shot in prayer circle, 22 cal. pistol, 2 rifles, 2 shotguns wrapped & taped in a quilt. No gun experience— only violent video games.	X	I	Front lobby	14	Mental illness; teacher was six yards away, returning from parking lot duty.
February 19, 1997. Bethel, AK. Evan Ramsey shoots 4. History of threats.	X	I	Lobby	16	Shotgun; revenge was motive.
February 2, 1996. Moses Lake, WA. Four shot	X	I	Algebra Class	14	During school; hunting rifle

Table 2-2

Expert Coding of Strategies and Interventions According to Their Likely Effectiveness in Reducing School Violence Incidents

What would have been most likely to make a difference? (Ranging from 0, least likely, to 3, most likely)	Primary prevention (universal) measures —behavior management curricula —schoolwide discipline	Secondary intervention (targeted) measures —individual and group intervention programs —parent training and support	CPTED measures	Police or security officers in the schools
Springfield, OR, assault in cafeteria.	1	3	3	2
St. Charles, MO, planned sniper attack, outdoors.	3	3	2	1
Onalaska, WA, boy takes girl off bus, shoots self at home.	1	3	0	0
Houston, TX, gun went off accidentally in backpack.	3	1	2	0
Fayetteville, TN, youth kills out of jealousy.	1	3	2	1
Pomona, CA, 3 shot after-hours, playing basketball.	2	3	1	0
Edinboro, PA, off-campus club.	1	3	0	0
Jonesboro, AR, 15 shot, false fire alarm.	2	3	2	1
West Paducah, KY, 8 shot in prayer circle.	1	3	2	1
Pearl, MS, 9 shot, possible "satanic" conspiracy by 6 kids.	2	3	3	2
Bethel, AK, Evan Ramsey shoots 4.	1	3	3	2

have a direct, positive impact. These ratings are broad-brush and subjective, but they do indicate priorities for possible remedial actions for the purpose of avoiding similar problems in the future.

Table 2-3 provides similar coding for generic situations that are often associated with violence in and around schools. This table further illustrates how circumstances can affect prioritization of remedial actions.

Through careful analysis of the locations of school tragedies, the circumstances surrounding them, and the motives behind the violence, CPTED experts obtain clues that can guide school officials in altering the nature and use of school spaces as one means to prevent such incidents in the future. By collecting data on and analyzing a broad range of similar situations, the CPTED knowledge base can be used to develop generic prevention strategies that until now have been largely unavailable.

Chapter 3 describes the CPTED knowledge base and how it has evolved over the last several decades.

Public Perception vs. Reality

Data and Polling in Context

Although school-related violence continues to be a grave concern, and incidents continue to occur, the pervasiveness of the problem needs to be kept in perspective.

40%—Decrease in school-related violent deaths, school year 1997/98 to 1998/99.

49%—Increase in poll respondents reporting fear of a school shooting in their community, 1998 to 1999.

1 in 2 million—The chance that a school-aged child would die in a school, 1998/99.

71%—Portion of respondents who thought such an incident was likely in their community.

56%—Decline in juvenile homicide arrests between 93 and 98.

62%—Portion of poll respondents who believe juvenile crime is increasing.

4%—Portion of juvenile homicides that occur in rural areas.

First—Rank of rural parents in fear for their children's safety in schools vs. urban and suburban parents.

Source: Justice Policy Institute/ Children's Law Center, April 24, 2000

www.cjcj.org/schoolhousehype/

Table 2-3

Generic Situations Coded for Likely Effectiveness in Terms of Responsiveness to Differing Strategies and Interventions

For the scenarios listed below, which remedies should take highest priority? (0-3)	Primary prevention (universal) measures	Secondary intervention (targeted) measures	CPTED measures	Police or security officers in schools
Crime-ridden neighborhood, reasonably behaved kids.	3	1	3	1
Reasonable neighborhood, out-of-control student body.	3	2	2	3
Good neighborhood and school, just a few out-of-control kids.	1	3	1	1
Crime-ridden neighborhood, out-of-control student body.	3	2	3	3
No problems of any kind, but area is becoming more diverse, and there are concerns that conflicts could occur.	3	0	1	0

0 = Least effective; 3 = Most effective

Thurston High School

On May 21, 1998, 15-year-old Kip Kinkel murdered his parents, then slipped onto his high school campus and shot into a crowded cafeteria, injuring twenty-five people and killing two. The incident was one of many high-profile mass school shootings in the United States within a relatively short period, and it drew considerable attention to Thurston High School, in Springfield, Oregon, as various parties sought explanations, remedies, or perhaps just someone to blame.

The school had no reason to assume a mass shooting would take place. It had no history of similar incidents, and generally did not have a significant problem with violent, intolerant, or abusive behavior.

A predictable residue of posttraumatic stress has affected many students and staff at the school since the shootings took place, but there has not been any indication of an escalation in violence at the school whatsoever. If anything, the opposite is true; the predominant attitude on campus from students and staff alike is that problems must be solved nonviolently. Kip Kinkel has not become an antihero among the disaffected. Rather, he is widely perceived as mentally ill.

With the benefit of hindsight, Kinkel's psychological problems are much more evident than they were at the time. His state of mind, coupled with easy access to deadly weapons and the failure of both his parents and the system as a whole to effectively intervene in time are now all patently obvious problems that should have been addressed. But on top of all those shortcomings, the facility itself, from a CPTED perspective, was an indefensible space.

Thurston's circumstances underscore the reality that schools can be found at two different ends of the spectrum, at least in the United States: those that perceive a continual problem with life-threatening violence and weapons violations, and are largely concentrated in blighted urban areas; and those that almost never see evidence of these types of problems, and that make up the vast majority of schools in the country.

For war-zone schools, the CPTED concept is an easy one to sell, but the application is difficult to finance. For relatively peaceful schools, CPTED changes may be looked upon as paranoid luxuries, wasting money that could be better spent on teachers and supplies. Paradoxically, as the wave of mass shootings has illustrated, it has been the low-risk schools, devoid of security features, that have suffered the most dramatic consequences.

The easy solution is to integrate CPTED into school designs when they are still in the blueprint stage, imposing little or no impact on the cost of the facility. More difficult is spending money after construction to mitigate security weaknesses that should have been caught earlier in the process. In too many cases, the original architecture is a dismal failure from a CPTED perspective, and the necessary improvements are significant financial investments.

Thurston High School is far from unique in this respect, but its story is illustrative. The school is vast and sprawling, with at least fourteen major uncontrolled access points, mostly in the form of dark, underlit breezeways, allowing entry into the facility.

Most of these entry points had no natural surveillance, territoriality, or access control incorporated into their design when the school was built in 1959. Mesh fences and gates were added to the breezeways a few years ago, but these are only secured after hours, primarily to prevent vandalism. They offer no protection for students during the school day.

Security cameras that view and tape the exterior of the building proved impotent as a deterrent or intervention tool during the Kinkel incident (see photo, page 56).

Making this site functional from a CPTED perspective would require the replacement of the mesh fences and gates at all fourteen access points with secure, controlled, and/or supervised entries. If cost were no concern, a high-security vestibule (see sidebar, page

Continued on p. 19

59) installed on each side of the building, along with conventionally secured entry points, would be ideal. Costs for four such entries could run as high as $360,000.

The school administrative office is located at the main entry point. The addition of a secure entry vestibule would not be architecturally difficult, but would only be worthwhile if the additional fourteen entry points were fully controlled.

The weakness of the overall design of this school cannot be overemphasized. Some critics might suggest that reasonable security arrangements could have compensated for the design flaws, but this would be an unfounded assumption. Consider the measures in place at the time of the shooting:

1. *Closed Campus*. Students in grades 9-11 cannot leave campus during the school day for any reason without parent and school permission. Even their cars are locked into the south lot. Seniors park in the north lot and their vehicles are not restricted.

2. *Building Security Cameras*. The entire perimeter of the building and courtyard is covered by security cameras 24 hours every day. The campus is also fenced to provide for restricted access and easier supervision of strangers on campus.

3. *Substitute/ Teacher/ Visitor Identification*. Visitors and substitutes are asked to check in at the office and wear identifying badges.

4. *Campus Monitor*. Two campus monitors patrol campus throughout the school day.

5. *Volunteers*. They assist with building supervision before school and during lunch, patrolling and talking to students.

6. *Cafeteria Supervision*. Two teachers are assigned each period throughout the day to walk around and monitor activity in the cafeteria.

7. *Campus Supervision*. Two teachers are assigned each period throughout the day to walk around and monitor activity on campus.

8. *2-Way Communication System*. All duty teachers, monitors, and administrators carry 2-way radios.

9. *Triage Committee*. Building administrators, counselors, and the school nurse meet weekly to review any student who has generated concerns by any member of the group. Problem solving takes place, and informal action plans are developed ranging from continued monitoring to intervention. This group also forms the primary crisis team for the building; specific roles in a crisis are reviewed with the group each fall.

10. *Safety Committee*. The building has a safety committee that meets monthly to review any safety concerns on campus. The committee is composed of classified staff, certified employees, and administration.

11. *Lockdown Procedure*. Building emergency procedures are reviewed with staff each fall and are contained in the staff handbook.

12. *Confidential Reporting System*. The school has an answering-machine system that allows individuals to leave messages for anyone during nonschool hours. The machine tape is reviewed each morning at 7:30 with messages distributed as necessary.

13. *Reward System*. A monetary reward system is in place and is used on a case-by-case basis, as deemed necessary by the administrator involved.

Since the time of the shooting, a School Resource Officer has been added to the mix. Beginning in spring 1999 all staff members have been required to wear picture ID badges when on campus.

Kip Kinkel's Route of Access, May 21, 1998, 0755 hours

1 Kinkel drove to a neighboring residential area and entered the grounds through an established pedestrian access point on the northeast corner of the property. A turnstile prevents vehicles from entering here. This access point sits in a vacant lot separated from neighboring residences by sight-obscuring fences and bushes. There is no natural surveillance in this direction from within any nearby or even distant buildings.

2 Kinkel threaded his way between cars in a small parking area and entered an unsecured breezeway on the north side of the property. His approach was captured by the surveillance camera, but nothing in his appearance appeared worthy of alarm at the time.

Continued on p. 21

3 Kinkel shot two students in the breezeway.

4 He then entered the cafeteria where the bulk of the shootings occurred. It was here that he was finally tackled and brought under control by fellow students.

CHAPTER
3
Key CPTED Concepts and Principles

*C*rime Prevention Through Environmental Design (CPTED) is built around three basic concepts:

1. **Natural surveillance**—the ability to see what's going on.
2. **Natural access control**—the ability to control entry and exit from an environment.
3. **Territoriality**—the ability of legitimate users to control an area, while discouraging illicit users.

CPTED takes a broad environmental view of a target setting, carefully noting structural design weaknesses and the extent to which they allow for potentially dangerous human behavior. When the physical design is faulty, or if the space is used inappropriately, CPTED seeks ways to redesign and use the space more effectively.

A cardinal rule in any CPTED evaluation of a particular space is to ask whether the space is used legitimately and in a functional manner. A number of CPTED recommendations will flow from the resulting analysis. The assumption is that the more functional a space becomes (that is, the more likely the space will be used for the purpose for which it was designed), the more likely it is that legitimate activity will occur there.

Use of school spaces for purposes other than those for which they were designed poses a common threat to school safety and security. Low-traffic areas on school campuses, such as bathrooms and stairways, par-

ticularly where there is a low ratio of adults to students, are examples of places vulnerable to criminal behavior and victimization. When CPTED principles and guidelines are implemented to make the school environment safer and more functional, crime prevention is often an important byproduct.

Here are some key principles of CPTED that are critical to the successful application of this process:

- Take the broadest possible view.
- Observe the physical setting and its relationship to human behavior in the setting.
- Notice any design weaknesses.
- Question everything.
- Look for ways to use the space more functionally, with the goal of encouraging desired behavior.
- Apply CPTED with integrity; if CPTED is skillfully applied, crime prevention will be a byproduct of its successful application.

CPTED practitioners design or redesign an overall environment so that it simply works better—deterring crime and undesired behavior in the process. CPTED takes all conventional security approaches into account: *mechanical* (the locks, structural changes, security technology), *human or organizational* (what people can do as individuals in using the space or as members of groups in order to be safer), and *natural measures*.

Natural measures are highly cost-effective in that, once instituted, they passively improve security. Installing a window or trimming a shrub, for example, can result in an improved capacity to monitor an environment without requiring conscious additional attention, and the benefit is often realized at a one-time-only cost.

Between "dead" walls and breezeways, this school has designed out natural surveillance and natural access control.

Contrast the effectiveness of these natural measures with hiring a security guard, which requires continued active attention and expenditure, or installing a security camera, which needs someone to actively watch the monitor. A key benefit of natural measures to a school, in this context, is that teachers and school staff can remain primarily focused on their normal duties, instead of on policing.

Natural Surveillance

An environment should be designed so legitimate users can see as much of it as possible without taking extra measures. For example, a window above the kitchen sink provides natural surveillance of the yard for anyone standing there. If the view from that window is obstructed, and a resident has to go to the front door to see what's happening outside, then natural surveillance is obviously impaired.

Solid walls or thick hedges on school campuses often serve no constructive purpose, but do provide "cover" (visual blockages that create locations in which unauthorized individuals can hide and engage in undesirable activities that are illegal, dangerous, or destructive).

Natural Access Control

The Anasazi cliff dwellings of the American Southwest allowed not only great natural surveillance but supreme access control as well. Visitors were subject to extensive scrutiny as they climbed ladders to gain entry to the Anasazi dwellings. Aside from the barrier provided by the natural physical structure, it was relatively easy for the residents to further impair access via physical resistance, a dropped rock, or other means.

In schools, access control typically means providing a gate keeper at any open door, sending all visitors to the main office for entry processing, and locking any doors that can't be watched. The distinction between *can not* and *may not* shouldn't be lost in this regard. *"May not"* is the proper description for many access-control policies, such as *"Visitors may not enter the school without obtaining a pass from the office."*

With such policies there is no device or means to enforce this rule on the *"can not"* level. The end result is a policy that will in-

The Use of Glass Reinforcement

Windows are critical for natural surveillance, but they do pose penetration risks. Glass breakage can provide access for burglars, but much worse is the fact that projectiles can penetrate windows and shattered glass can cause serious injuries, particularly when explosions are involved.

Glass reinforcement can be very expensive, so its use in schools will of course be extremely limited. Reinforcement options, in order of expense, include the following:

• **Security film.** This material is a thin film usually installed on the inside of the glass. If the glass is shattered, it is still difficult to penetrate; the film holds the glass together. In most cases the film is a sufficient deterrent. Burglars will still succeed at breaking the window, but they are less likely to gain entry. Costs run close to $5 per square foot including installation. Some types of film are also touted for use on the exterior of the pane, designed to absorb vandalism that aims at scratching the window. The film is eventually peeled off and replaced with a new layer.

• **Frame reinforcement.** Security film by itself may not provide enough protection against explosive devices. If a higher level of security is desired, the filmed window can be reinforced with specially designed L-shaped frame reinforcers that hold the film firmly against the edges of the pane and keep the window from blowing inward.[1]

• **Laminated glass-clad polycarbonates.** This involves laminating high-tech polycarbonate plastics to glass, or in some cases not using glass at all. This product is highly resistant to penetration and should deter molotov cocktails and the like, at a cost of approximately $50 per square foot.

• **Bullet-resistant glass.** At 1-2" thick, this multiple-ply laminate of alternating glass and polycarbonate and/or metal mesh hybrids will "resist" bullets "ranging from a .38 super automatic to a high power .30-06 rifle,"[2] but at a cost of about $150 per square foot.

---

[1]Details on this type of product can be seen on the web at: www.framelok.com/usa/system or at www.framegard.co.uk/story/fulstory.htm

[2]www.saflex.com/Application

---

convenience the vast majority of school visitors but that can be ignored by willful trespassers. Policies move to the *"can not"* level when trespassing without a pass is physically impossible, because the doors just won't open, or somebody's there to stop trespassers.

The key point is that school officials should consider the potential impact of *any* security measures before their implementation and ask, "Is this going to have the intended effect on targeted behavior or does it merely convey proper etiquette to students and others who are already willing to vol-untarily comply?" An armed intruder is unlikely to turn away from a doorway just because it's marked *"Do not enter,"* which is a *"may not"* level of control. Locking and carefully monitoring the door, on the other hand, could make a considerable difference at the *"can not"* level.

Territorial Behavior

The third key element of CPTED is *territoriality*. Gang members understand this concept very well—they use graffiti to spray and mark areas they wish to claim as their turf. By painting over their graffiti, we sym-

Access-Control Devices

Keys are often troublesome. They get copied and lost, and rekeying or coping is expensive. Staff members are obligated to carry rings of keys to open doors.

Keys do have some advantages. They are not dependent on an external power source being operable. There will still be a need to have keys available in a highly secure location in case of a power-outage if it affects an entry system.

There are several good alternatives to keys. These include push-button codes, swipe cards, proximity cards, and fingerprint or retinal scanners. Push-button coded entries are vulnerable because uninvited visitors can in many cases learn the codes. Each time the code is changed, everyone has to be informed about the change.

Swipe cards are an improvement because the card itself is coded to allow entry to only appropriate doors at selected times. Only one card is needed for multiple entry points, and the card can double as an identification card. Even better than a swipe card, which involves placing the card in a machine, is the proximity card, which only has to be close to the reader to unlock a door.

It is a good idea for schools to get bids or cost estimates on switching to these devices. Even if no change is planned for the immediate future, there may come a time when the cost of rekeying, and the amount of theft and burglary, warrant making the switch.

Contact: Check with a local member of the National Fire and Burglar Alarm Association for estimates. You can also check with manufacturers, such as Cypress Computer Systems at 800-807-2977, or ILCO (which produces LearnLok) at www.ilcounican.com, telephone: 888-217-5654.

bolically take that territory back, which sends a very important message to everyone. If a school can reinforce a sense of territoriality and shared ownership, students and staff will feel more empowered to challenge inappropriate behavior when it occurs.

Maintenance of school property (for example, picking up trash, fixing broken windows, or sweeping up broken bottles) sends a strong message that this is a school someone cares about. Well-maintained, graffiti-free areas are treated with more respect by students and communicate a sense of safety, caring, and effectiveness.

School activities can similarly reinforce territoriality. If the ball field is used for Little League games on weekends, it won't be attractive to criminals looking for victims, gangs seeking to claim turf, or addicts dealing drugs. It will be harder for such groups to intimidate the general populace because citizens are present in large numbers and will likely have plenty of assistance resources (such as cell phones).

How should territoriality operate within the context of a diverse student body? In schools, especially high schools, students seek to establish territoriality in a multitude of ways, from their allegiance to the school's athletic teams to their mode of dress and the places they choose to congregate during lunch breaks.

Expressing territoriality in these ways can foster a strong sense of belonging and commitment to the school; but if school officials allow measures to be taken without a sufficiently broad perspective, they can unintentionally undermine inclusiveness. Different cultures, religions, races, beliefs, lifestyles, or genders can be at odds when the accommodation of one comes at the expense of others.

Sensitivity to and accommodation of differences are important considerations in achieving *balanced territoriality*. The alter-

Examples of Territoriality That Lead to Exclusion

Men's team: the Spartans Women's team: the Spartanettes.	The diminutive ending is just what the term suggests—diminishing, or making less of something.
Annual "slave auction"—people bid on other people for services, as a fundraiser.	For cultures with a collective or individual memory of enslavement, this can be a chilling trivialization of a culture's history.
Football team name: the Cherokees or the Redskins.	Naming a team after a culture other than one's own may not feel offensive—but what if the team were named after your culture, and the team members didn't belong to your culture? What if the name implied that your culture was savage or warlike?
An extreme emphasis on one school activity, while disregarding another.	If the primary message apparent at the school is "our team is best, kill all the rest," how does this instill pride in non-athletes or students who didn't make the team? How about students who transferred from a competing team's school? Does this message reinforce curriculum that promotes tolerance and respect for others?

native can be an enhanced sense of ownership by a mainstream subpopulation of students, but a deeper sense of alienation among at-risk students or minority groups. In this case, territoriality for one group is gained at the price of another group's exclusion.

Ultimately this sense of exclusion can exacerbate problem behaviors at school, as one set of students express intolerance of other students, and they in turn lose commitment to and respect for the school. Students looking for a place to belong, who feel rejected by a mainstream group's message of territoriality, may drift into gangs or other undesirable circles.

These three concepts—natural surveillance, natural access control, and territoriality—can be brought to bear productively when assessing the vast majority of troubled

physical environments. If carefully considered, they can help pinpoint significant environmental design problems and weaknesses that can be remedied. In many cases, when CPTED considerations are applied at the design stage of a new school building, security can be greatly improved at no additional cost in construction or retrofitting.

Enduring CPTED solutions can be as simple as moving a window to improve natural surveillance, changing a fence design to establish access control, or painting a mural to build a sense of pride and ownership among students, while simultaneously recovering turf claimed by gangs.

Design Conflict

Errors in the way an area or setting is structurally designed, situated, or used can provide evidence of a dysfunctional environment. For example, at the onset of World War II, New York City ordered that all skylights be painted over to reduce the amount of light visible to enemy planes. So the skylights became dysfunctional—and stayed that way until very recently, when someone thought to question the situation. New York's Plaza Hotel was less fortunate: the hotel operators reportedly painted over

Wrought-iron fencing provides access control while maintaining natural surveillance.

some Tiffany style skylights and then installed a large air conditioning system that blocked the skylights permanently.

This example underscores a basic rule of CPTED: *question everything.* Why is an environment designed the way it is? Why does one segment of the community avoid meetings at the school? Why do people use that passageway, but not another? Why is this door propped open? Perhaps a particular building, room, or entryway previously served one function but now serves another.

How is space defined? Is it clear who owns it? Where are its borders? Borders can be so unclear that they actually invite trespassers by default; for example, there's nothing telling them not to intrude, and it may look like a good place to explore, or sleep, or to sell drugs. In some settings, signs can help where the environmental design falls short. Clear, reasonable, well-communicated rules and restrictions help encourage appropriate behavior on the property or in the facility.

Safety concerns can paralyze a school's ability to focus on its primary function of providing instruction that leads to student learning. Some remedies, such as hiring security guards, can be quite costly. Utilizing school staff to patrol the grounds reduces the amount of time they have available for their primary educational roles. Overt security measures, such as armed guards, metal detectors, and random backpack or locker checks, may actually be counterproductive if they reinforce fearfulness on campus.

By applying CPTED concepts effectively, a school can (1) improve natural surveillance, access control, and territoriality, often with minimal, one-time investments that can be incorporated into bond measures or facility-construction budgets; (2) save money by reducing the need for more active, ongoing measures, such as hiring security guards; and (3) create an environment that reinforces the primary purpose of an educational facility.

Communication Devices

Communication devices are good investments. Unlike video cameras or armed guards, they do not "up the ante" in raising the level of fear based on their presence. Instead, they facilitate the reporting of suspicious or threatening activity, and they make it easier for the school's administration to send emergency messages quickly. Disasters can at least be mitigated in almost all cases with good communication. Options include:

Public-address systems and intercoms. These should be checked at least annually to see if they still work, including during inclement weather. For example, in some schools, the intercoms don't work when it rains! It should be possible to hear announcements in the bathrooms, the cafeteria, the parking lot, and throughout the grounds. It should be possible to reach all locations with one announcement as well as selected rooms.

Telephones. There should be a phone in each room. Better still, provide staff with cell phones. Combination cell phone/radios provide more flexibility. If at all possible, phones should be equipped with caller ID—a very helpful feature in identifying prank callers.

Display pagers. These devices can be very useful for quietly sending emergency messages and updates simultaneously to large numbers of staff. The proper setup includes a keyboard that can be used to enter and send messages to anyone carrying a pager. It can send to specific individuals, specific teams (such as a crisis-response group), or to all staff. One of the scariest elements of a major crisis involves being barricaded and not knowing what's going on. This device could be very effective in dispelling some of those fears by sending regular updates, such as the location of a gunman, whether police have arrived yet, and so forth.

Followup: Check with local Pager companies to see if this service is available in your area. One company that provides this product in selected Oregon locations is PageNet at 503-821-2035.

Tracking devices. In some cases tracking devices may be appropriate. These can be carried, serving as portable panic buttons, and monitored for location within the site by a central computer. These devices can also be attached to valuable equipment to track thefts in progress.

Followup: Check with local security companies for this service. One manufacturer is Detection Systems, Inc.: telephone 716-223-4060, www.detectionsys.com.

CHAPTER
4

Site Evaluation:
The Foundation for Improving
School Safety and Security

*E**very school can benefit from an assessment of its environmental design to determine whether the school is a safe and secure place to learn and work. A school site surrounded by or infused with criminal activity has an obvious need for such an assessment, but even campuses that seem at first glance to be orderly and secure may, when inspected, be found to present a multitude of risks.*

This recycling and garbage area includes a tank of flammable gas. Options would include either full exposure or full enclosure. Either option would discourage arson.

It takes only one tragedy to make the benefits of preventive assessment crystal clear in hindsight for any school. Even relatively minor environmental flaws are worthy of attention and action. For example, if someone trips over broken steps because of deferred maintenance, that's a twisted ankle, and serious litigation may result. If nothing is done to actively discourage drug dealers from hanging out on school campuses, the district incurs a risk of liability that may threaten its insurability. A child who threatens violent behavior obviously cannot be

ignored. Whenever there is a history of trouble, or if future problems are foreseeable, one can reasonably anticipate eventual personal injuries, as well as subsequent legal action.

This chapter presents a variety of tools for assessing school safety and recommends procedures for conducting the school-site evaluation.

Initial Assessment on Self-Report Instruments

To determine the general level of risk in a school and its surrounding community, the National School Safety Center's School Crime Assessment Tool (see Appendix A) and the Oregon School Safety Survey (see Appendix B) can serve as good initial indicators.

To examine the need for Crime Prevention Through Environmental Design (CPTED) measures, see the *8-Point CPTED Needs Assessment* (page 32), along with the *Campus Incident Frequency and Severity Scale* (page 33).

Schools do not exist in a vacuum but rather are a reflection of the contexts in which they function. Surrounding circumstances and risks (for example, neighborhood and student and family characteristics) can obviously positively or negatively affect a school's overall level of risk for violence. The self-report assessment tools provided in Appendices A and B can help quantify some of these mediating factors.

Administrators who are implementing a CPTED assessment must consider a number of issues and characteristics of their school and its community. Such considerations include, but are not limited to, the following:

- **What is the student-teacher ratio?** The greater the ratio of students to teachers

Extensive hate graffiti undermines school climate and territoriality.

and other adults in the school, the larger the overall risk to school safety. Students consistently report that the more adults there are in school spaces, especially low-

Eight-Point CPTED Needs Assessment

1. Can students travel from home to school without encountering unreasonable obstacles?

2. Do areas directly adjoining school property have legitimacy, positive territoriality, and ownership (as opposed to a no-man's land where snipers could hide)?

3. Can office staff see intruders approaching the building at any given time without taking extraordinary measures?

4. Does the school have the ability to stop unwelcome visitors, such as armed students or menacing adults, from simply choosing to enter the school? (That is, must they ring a bell, pass through a metal detector, pass the main office window, be buzzed in, check a backpack, or just be visible to staff so that they can be challenged? Or can they decide to enter through the back door, the side door, the kitchen door, or other place?)

5. Do staff members have natural surveillance of activity inside the school, without having to step into the hallway, through a set of double doors, or around a corner?

6. Can staff rapidly lock down the school, with students protected in individual classrooms, in case an armed person has entered the building? (That is, is there a working public-address system, and can the classroom doors be quickly locked?)

7. Does the school's overall climate and atmosphere, as reflected in what occurs on a daily basis (including security measures, orderliness, cooperation, and teacher morale), inspire hope, confidence, appreciation, trust, and respect among students and staff?

The correct answer, in items 1-7, should be yes. If it isn't, School CPTED analysis should be strongly considered.

8. Are there locations at the school—hallways, bathrooms, hidden alcoves, dugouts, locker rooms, loading docks, informal gathering areas—that you associate with ongoing problems, such as graffiti, vandalism, bullying, or worse activities? (If yes, see Campus Incident Frequency and Severity Scale)

Campus Incident Frequency and Severity Scale

This exercise is intended to quickly identify problem areas in the school, based on your *general* impressions. Rate each item for frequency and severity:

Frequency

Estimated frequency/ past 12 months (include anecdotes, rumors, informal, and/or formal reports):

0—No problems, not applicable.

1—At least three incidents have occurred in the past school year.

2—Problems occur at least monthly.

Severity / past 12 months:

0—Inconsequential/ not applicable.

1—Property damage or theft under $100, and/or low-risk extensive littering, such as cigarette butts and paper cups.

2—Property damage or theft over $100; and/or high-risk debris such as broken bottles, hypodermic needles, bullets, knives, and/or other weapons.

3—Verbal conflict (such as sexual or racial harassment), disruptive behavior (yelling in class, throwing books, overt defiance such as breaking rules in front of staff).

4—Unarmed physical conflict, fear-inducing behavior.

5—Armed physical conflict.

Location	Total Frequency (rate 0-2)	Severity (rate 0-5)
1. classrooms		
2. hallway locker bays		
3. locker rooms		
4. gym		
5. bathrooms (specify male/female)		
6. other specific indoor areas (such as library, computer lab, woodshop)		
7. specific *undefined* outdoor areas (such as behind bushes)		
8. specific *defined* outdoor areas (such as loading dock or playground)		
9. parking areas		
10. bike or foot paths		
11. nearby loitering locations		
12. nearby businesses, malls, or plazas		
13. nearby residences		
14. campuswide, other (specify) or unknown location		
15. locations associated with particular groups / gangs		
TOTALS		

A frequency of at least 2 and severity of at least 2 at any one location warrant attention. The higher the total, the more urgent the need.

traffic areas, the safer they feel and the less opportunity there is for victimization by others.

- **What are some distinctive features of the student-body population**? These might include the number of students on reduced-fee or free lunches; the migration or turnover rate for the student body as a whole; the number of discipline referrals, suspensions, and expulsions within a school year; and the number of students who have been arrested. Are there conflicts among diverse groups within the school?

Open campuses are more frequently associated with off campus conflict.

- **Is the campus open or closed?** If students are free to wander on and off campus during the school day, there may be implications for traffic conflicts, neighborhood problems, drug usage and dealing, as well as the continual risk of weapons being brought back onto the campus. An open campus often serves as a risk factor for unsafe schools.

- **What is the school's overall climate?** What measures are in place to affect it? Are there universal violence-prevention curricula and interventions in place (such as the Second Step Violence Prevention Program, the Effective Behavioral Support Program, and so forth)? Does schoolwide discipline exist and is it effective?

- **What percentage of the student body displays excessive antisocial behavior?** How many referrals are there to the office per week or per month? Individually, what are the consequences for student misbehavior and conflict? Are there targeted intervention programs available for at-risk students such as First Steps to Success (Walker and others 1997)? Are staff

responses to student misbehavior uniform and consistent? Is there a system for communicating about student behavior among staff? Are classified employees left out of the loop, or included? Are police officers assigned to the schools and, if so, for how many hours a week? What are their roles? How effective are the police at preventing crimes, gathering intelligence, or apprehending suspects? Do they have a role other than enforcement, such as law-related counseling or education? Is the police presence having an impact? How well are the police received by the students? Has anyone ever polled students to find out?

- **How often have the police been dispatched to the school? Is crime at the school a chronic problem or an unusual occurrence?** Cooperative police agencies with computerized databases can be an enormous help in answering these questions. How do the statistics for this school compare with those of similar schools elsewhere in the community, and with the community as a whole, on a per-capita basis? How does crime within the school compare with crime within a four-block radius of the school? During what hours do most crimes in the surrounding area occur? Are students walking through a war zone to get to campus? How many students from a particular school have been detained by the juvenile justice system this year?

- **Have there been traumatic recent events or are there smoldering, long-term community tensions that need to be considered?** Has there been a recent school shooting publicized in the media? Has there been a rash of bike thefts or vandalism? Is there a developing problem with bullying on the playground? Have businesses nearby been fighting a wave of robberies?

- **Are there resources to be accessed in the surrounding neighborhood?** Are there businesses that can be partnered with? Are youth mentors to be found? Are libraries, parks, swimming pools, greenhouses, museums, or exhibits available nearby? Are there natural features that can be incorporated into science classes, such as streams, fields, or gardens? If the neighborhood is in terrible shape, or if students have to walk through a "war zone" or high-speed traffic area to get to school, then the school may want to consider working with community leaders and investing in the surrounding area's renewal. Schools might also consider involving the students in transforming their neighborhoods, helping small businesses repair damaged storefronts, cleaning up vacant lots, or starting microbusinesses such as herb gardens. School safety often reflects the level of safety in the surrounding neighborhood.

Any decisions about changing the school environment will benefit substantially from an indepth understanding of neighborhood and community assets and deficits. The risks found in the surrounding neighborhood, par-

ticularly risks identified through use of the school-safety assessment tools (see Appendices A and B), the eight-point CPTED Needs Assessment, or the Campus Incident Frequency and Severity Scale will go far in identifying the school's risks and vulnerabilities.

It may become clear, for example, that the playground is a frequent trouble spot and the location lacks natural surveillance. Students approaching from the south side of the building, for example, may be chronically late because trains frequently block the road, gangs menace students, or traffic lights don't work reliably. The hallway at lunch hour may be the scene of many conflicts because of foot traffic in and out of the cafeteria conflicting with students' socializing in locker bays at the same time. The more specifically such problems are defined, the greater the likelihood that solutions will be on target, efficient, and workable. This sort of analysis should be part of an assessment of a school's safety status and capacity for positive change.

School Environmental Design Assessment

Assessment of school facilities for the purpose of improving safety can be an unwieldy and difficult task. The old one-room schoolhouse has generally grown into either a two-story labyrinth in a fortress-like shell or a sprawling hodgepodge of buildings scattered over a large site in a typical campus-style setting. For the vast majority of these facilities, CPTED principles were absent when the architects did their design work. The end result is that retrofitting, often on a large scale, is now necessary if the school is to be even marginally safe.

Who should perform the assessment? Factoring in time, money, and available expertise, school districts might choose between hiring a CPTED consultant or conducting the assessment in-house. One of the goals of this chapter is to equip school staffs to conduct their own assessments and learn how to interpret the results. Districts can send one or more employees to an institute for CPTED training, hire a CPTED specialist to provide a seminar locally, or, most economically, use the remainder of this chapter as a guide to conduct a self-evaluation.

Guidelines for Conducting a CPTED Evaluation

Once an initial assessment of the school's relative safety has been completed using the self-report measures described in the preceding section, the CPTED evaluation process can begin. Several forms and checklists are essential tools with which to conduct the security inspection and evaluation. Readers have our permission to duplicate or adapt these forms as needed to gain the greatest benefit from the evaluation.

1. The School Environmental Design Assessment (SEDA) Cover Sheet. To begin the process, the CPTED evaluator fills out this form, which assembles on one sheet vital information about the school for quick overview purposes. A blank sample (for reproduction) of this form is provided on page 38. To illustrate the intended use of the SEDA cover sheet, a completed form, using a hypothetical school as an example, is provided on page 39.

2. The CPTED Site-Assessment Form. This two-page form is used to record observations on characteristics of particular places, such as a single classroom, a hallway, a playground, or a site in the surrounding community that is frequented by students. The evaluator can also record recommendations and rate the relative risk to security of the conditions he or she identifies.

A blank copy of the Site-Assessment Form is provided on page 40, along with a sample of the completed form (for a hypothetical school) on the following page.

It is not critical that every room or nook and cranny be treated to its own assessment form. Some rooms or hallways will have no apparent problems; in such cases, the evaluator can check them off on the Location Checklist on page 42 and move on.

In column three of the Site-Assessment Form, the evaluator ranks (on a scale of 0 to 3) the relative risk status of each design feature of the school location being assessed. These ratings are based on the documented evidence at hand and follow a simple, four-step hierarchy of risk:

- No risk, where the design looks acceptable and no problems have been reported, is valued at 0.

- Low risk, where the design looks weak but there have been no reported problems, rates 1.

- Medium risk, where the design looks weak and there is clear evidence or reports of trouble, rates 2.

- High risk, where serious design flaws are apparent and/or have contributed to serious consequences, rates 3.

The risks are tallied for each location within the school and its surroundings. When the CPTED assessment is complete, a reviewer can quickly determine where to focus remedial or preventive actions. Each location within the site can earn a total rating of anywhere from 0 to 9. Obviously, a 9 rating warrants immediate attention.

The key words listed in the left-hand column of this form, under the categories Surveillance, Access Control, and Territoriality/Climate, are included only as prompts. Most items will not be relevant to every location within the site, and it is not required that they be addressed or rated. They are included only as reminders to help the evaluator consider possible points of concern and/or conceivable remedies. The list of prompts is not exhaustive; valid remedies can be designed that are not noted on this list.

The key words in the prompts list are defined in the following section, and many of the terms are discussed in greater detail in the subsequent section, Conducting the School-Site Evaluation. If you encounter unfamiliar terminology on the form, consult the corresponding discussion of the terms that follows.

3. Location Checklist. The evaluator uses this form (on page 42) to keep track of which locations within and around the campus have been scrutinized. One copy should suffice; using this checklist in conjunction with multiple copies of the Site-Assessment Form, the evaluator checks off locations as they are inspected. The "comments" section of the form provides an opportunity for brief reminders, such as "Asbestos abatement in progress. Come back after 3/24," "No problems apparent here," or "Scheduled to be remodeled for a band practice area summer of 2000."

Discussion of Terms on the Site-Evaluation Form: Problems to Watch for and Related Solutions

In this section, we define and clarify terms on the CPTED Site-Assessment Form. The following discussion of terminology (in alphabetical order) corresponds to the prompts found on the survey sheet and provides sample problems and solutions.

Abutting areas—Two or more activities may overlap or combine with dangerous results. For example, if bus exhaust is inadvertently aimed at the air-conditioning intake pipes, the consequences can be serious. Remedies include examining adjacent activities for compatibility, moving one of the activities, or separating them with dividing structures.

Activity Placement—At times, activities are poorly located on a school site. Placing a basketball court next to a sand box can cause collisions between basketball players and toddlers. A playground placed next to a machine shop can expose children to unnecessary hazards. On the other hand, moving a legitimate activity into an area can be a good remedy, pushing potential misbehavior away from a location.

Alarm systems—Many schools utilize alarm systems but may lack a clear understanding of how they operate. Often alarms are old and poorly designed, or fail to identify which part of the building is registering smoke, noise, or glass breakage. Remedies include offering inservice training, conducting drills or practice scenarios, and checking with the alarm company or police to see how accurately the alarm pinpoints a problem location.

Alternative entries—Do visitors have too many entry options? Are you focusing on the front door while the back door is wide open? Remedies include considering all points of possible entry, as discussed under Gateways below.

Annunciators—Schools with dozens of doors have a hard time keeping track of them all. Electronic annunciators can set off an LED display or a buzzer at a main office console, identifying which door has been opened. These devices are particularly useful after hours, or when tighter security is warranted.

Beneath building areas—Problem visitors may be able to access a school through a crawl space beneath the building. Make sure those areas are sealed off.

Blind corners—If activity around the corner is out of sight, pedestrians can't prepare themselves for what they may be about to encounter. These are common problems

School Environmental
Design Assessment Cover Sheet

Name of School _____

Location _____

Contact name and number _____

Date _____

Total student population _____

Total staff _____

Distinctive features of student body population (demographics, special needs, language, free lunch, turnover, etc.)

Open or closed campus _____

Universal measures _____

Targeted measures _____

Crisis plan access _____

Police or security guards on campus _____

Recent events or other issues of concern _____

_____

Condition of Public Address System, indoors and outdoors _____

_____

Hot spots/ primary issues _____

_____

Calls for police service at school, 12-month period_____

Calls for police service, 4-block radius, 12-month period _____

School Environmental
Design Assessment Cover Sheet
(completed sample)

Name of School: Ridley High School

Location: 702 Pearl Road

Contact name and number: Head custodian, Jack Webb, 333-3333, and Principal, Ginger Rodeknik, 333-4545

Date: 4/23/99

Total student population: 987

Total staff: 35

Distinctive features of student body population *(demographics, special needs, language, free lunch, turnover, etc.)*: 60% Black, 30% Hispanic, 10% White

Open or closed campus: closed

Universal measures: school rule book handed out in September; violence prevention curricula being considered by a committee of teachers.

Targeted measures: Problem students are referred to the special-services team for individual behavior-management planning.

Crisis plan access: The school crisis plan is on the principal's wall, and should be on each classroom wall.

Police or security guards on campus: Officer Pat Ridley is assigned to four schools in this section of town. He is at this school on Mondays, or if called because of a crisis. He carries a pager.

Recent events or other issues of concern: Gang graffiti persistently showing up behind the gym; Mr. Webb reports finding broken bottles and condoms on the gym roof on a regular basis.

Public address system: Doesn't work in playground, sometimes fails indoors when it rains.

Hot spots/ primary issues: Ms. Rodeknik describes three students as "scary," including one who has a family that has threatened violence against her for disciplining him. The father is known to carry a knife and has a drinking problem.

Calls for police service at school, 12-month period: *(These data may be available from local police agencies, depending on their technical resources—computerized data bases, crime analysts, adequate time and budgets, and ultimately their willingness to cooperate)* 62

Calls for police service, 4-block radius, 12-month period: 870

Site-Assessment Form

Area:	Observations/Recommendations	Risk 0-3*

Surveillance
· lights
· landscaping
· windows
· obstructions to sight or
  sound
· traffic related
· dead walls
· blind corners
· blind alcoves
· mirrors
· cameras
· activity placement

Access Control
· fortress
· sprawl
· gateways
· traffic control
· fencing
· zones
· beneath building
· roof access
· alternative entries
· door and key controls
· annunciators
· windows
· alarm systems
· public events
· bathrooms
· water fountains
· emergency vehicles

Territoriality/Climate
· gang indicators
· other messages
· signs
· gathering areas
· patios
· maintenance
· safe materials
· abutting areas
· furnishings/decor

TOTAL

* Risk values: 0=no apparent risk; 1=low risk; 2=medium risk, evidence of misbehavior; 3=high risk, major design flaws and/or serious problems.

** Key words in the left-hand column are prompts to help guide site evaluations. They are not necessarily relevant to every location.

Site-Assessment Form
(completed sample)

Area: North grounds	Observations/Recommendations	Risk 0-3*
Surveillance · lights · landscaping · windows · obstructions to sight or sound · traffic related · dead walls · blind corners · blind alcoves · mirrors · cameras · activity placement	Mostly dead walls from school side. Limited visibility from neighbors and corner store. Can we put in windows? Lights at night cause glare; neighbors can't really see what's going on. May have made a difference in recent assault—neighbors were unable to determine what they were hearing. Maybe shield the lights?	1 3
Access Control · fortress · sprawl · gateways · traffic control · fencing · zones · beneath building · roof access · alternative entries · door and key controls · annunciators · windows · alarm systems · public events · bathrooms · water fountains · emergency vehicles	There's nothing to keep cars from entering the field. In an accident a car could come over curb and onto baseball field. A drunk driver did so last term and a child was injured. Plant trees, or install fencing?	3
Territoriality/Climate · gang indicators · other messages · signs · gathering areas · patios · maintenance · safe materials · abutting areas · furnishings/decor	The bathrooms were locked. Are they opened for games? The landscaping nearby is in bad shape and is collecting garbage. Racial epithets have been painted on the storage shed. Trim shrubs, make arrangements to open bathrooms, repaint shed?	2
TOTAL		9

* Risk values: 0=no apparent risk; 1=low risk; 2=medium risk, evidence of misbehavior; 3=high risk, major design flaws and/or serious problems.

** Key words in the left-hand column are prompts to help guide site evaluations. They are not necessarily relevant to every location.

Location Checklist

Location Checklist (Use in conjunction with Site–Assessment Form. Check off locations once they've been examined.)

✔	Location	Comments
	Surrounding neighborhood (N,S,E,W)	
	Borders and grounds (N,S,E,W)	
	Building exterior (N,S,E,W)	
	Playgrounds	
	Parking lots	
	Driveways	
	Loading docks, dumpsters	
	Main entry area	
	Main office	
	Hallways and all entry/exit doors	
	Classrooms	
	Cafeteria	
	Gymnasium	
	Auditorium	
	Bathrooms	
	Locker rooms	
	Art rooms	
	Industrial and home economics rooms	
	Science labs	
	Library	
	Preschool	
	Courtyards	
	Music rooms	
	Special-education rooms	
	Computer / technology rooms	
	Furnace and custodial storage	
	Time-out room	
	Meeting / conference rooms	

in hallways, where students may collide, or outdoors, where bullies may lie in wait for victims to appear. Common remedies include installing convex mirrors, moving walkways a few feet further away from the building (to expand the view at the corner), or redesigning a hallway with a curved or chamfered design.

Cameras—When no other surveillance options are feasible, cameras may be a reasonable consideration. Fire stairwells, secluded basements, poorly designed sprawling buildings, or other strategic locations on campuses may be most effectively observed with video cameras. However, recognize that cameras are usually more effective for gathering evidence after the fact than they are as a tool for discouraging misbehavior. Their quality can vary dramatically, from impressive to useless. Cameras need to be connected to a slow-speed VCR for taping purposes and/or watched on monitors.

Dead walls—This refers to solid walls that lack windows. Long, dead walls generally offer "cover," or a place to hide, for people engaged in illicit activities. The more dead walls at a location, the harder it is to see activity on the grounds from inside, and the more dependent a school becomes on patrols and/or surveillance cameras. Obvious remedies involve either installing windows or redesigning the walls to allow surveillance. The walls could be reduced to three feet in height, constructed from wrought iron, replaced with a rose trellis, or demolished as unnecessary.

Door and key controls—In what manner are doors secured? Are keys used, and if so, how well are they controlled? Are they frequently copied and handed out? Does anyone know who has keys? Are alternative entries controlled with alarms? Do doors lock automatically upon closing? Do the automatic closers work? Remedies include switching to coded entries, using smart cards, marking keys "do not duplicate," installing fire alarms on emergency doors, and maintaining existing hardware.

Emergency vehicles—Do improved security arrangements block emergency vehicle access? Remedies include communicating with emergency vehicle personnel about key or electronic gate-access arrangements.

Fencing—Would more fencing at this location make a difference? Or does the type of fencing have implications for safety and security? Is it serving as a dead wall? Is it easy to climb over? Does it pose a liability risk due to dangerous design features, such as voltage, barbs, or tips? Is it covered with graffiti? Remedies involve changing to a more appropriate fence design or material, such as wrought iron, which is highly vandal resistant and provides little surface area for graffiti.

Fortress—Some buildings, including large chain stores, exclusive communities, and schools, wall themselves in to enhance security. The weakness in this approach is that it leaves people outside the walls, including students, exposed and without protection. In worst-case scenarios, people inside the walls cannot hear, see, or reach people outside the walls to provide assistance, or vice versa. In a school, this can mean that a child is at higher risk than ever while traveling to and from school. Remedies include installing windows, removing unneeded walls, installing cameras or mirrors, transporting by bus, or deploying crossing guards and other security personnel.

Furnishings/decor—Does the school decor reinforce messages of pride and belonging? If the school looks uncomfortable, feels uncomfortable, or sends a message that alienates, its appearance is subverting the school's mission. Remedies include involving students and their families in room decoration and furniture selection.

Gang indicators—Gang graffiti is a common indicator, but clothing styles and police reports can also provide evidence. Gang activity is a strong indicator that a location is at high risk. Remedies include implementing gang-intervention programs, moving activities to safer locations, improving surveillance, or displacing gang activity by moving in legitimate non-gang activities.

Gateways—How many access points are there? Metal detectors at the front door are worthless if intruders can enter through the service entrance, or slip a gun through an open window. Sporting events will lose income if visitors have the option of slipping under the tent. Remedies include tighter security at alternative access points, more fencing, better key control, and stricter policies about open doors.

Gathering areas—Where do people assemble and for what purposes? Has the back lot turned into a skateboard park? Do students gather to buy drugs behind the corner grocery store? Remedies include redesigning areas to be conducive to desired activities while discouraging undesirable actions, improving natural surveillance, or blocking off access. Developed gathering areas will attract legitimate activity, leaving illegitimate activity isolated and more apparent.

Landscaping—Do trees, bushes, shrubbery, or ground contours block the view? Remedies may include lopping off lower tree limbs, reducing shrubs to no more than three feet in height, or bulldozing mounds.

Lights—Is lighting adequate? Are there pockets of shadow? Does the lighting create glare? Remedies may include changing, installing, protecting, or redirecting light fixtures.

Maintenance—Site designs can be excellent, but poor maintenance can undermine their effectiveness. If trash is accumulating at a particular spot, or if graffiti is al-

lowed to remain on a wall, the school is effectively ceding control over that area. Buildings that are falling apart similarly send a message that the school is giving up. The remedy is effective, timely maintenance.

Mirrors—Any location with blind spots may benefit from the installation of mirrors. These may be commercial convex mirrors, or they may be reflective aluminum sculpture that helps expose otherwise hidden activity. Mirrors are one of the most economical CPTED remedies available.

Obstructions to sight or sound— Does anything block vision or the ability to hear activity? Obstructions could include sculptures, landscaping, walls, abandoned tool sheds, construction noise that makes teaching nearly impossible, or double-door vestibules that are designed to block sound. Remedies may include moving objects, razing eyesores, installing mirrors, or mounting acoustic buffering materials.

Other messages—Has the school or have surrounding businesses installed signs that send productive or destructive messages? How do these messages hurt or help the school's mission? Do they frighten and alienate, or encourage and inspire? Remedies include petitioning adult bookstores to hide offensive materials, or helping schools to craft more inclusive messages in their entry areas.

Patios—School rooms often have small sections of underutilized grounds just outside their windows, but the rooms have no individual ownership of that space. Disruptive behavior can fill the void. One remedy would be to develop the area as a patio or garden area, establishing classroom turf.

Public events—School security arrangements may be adequate during the school day, but may fall short during public events. Gym or auditorium events, for example, may oblige the school to allow visitors access to the entire building. Remedies include considering the impact of public events and adjusting access design and control accordingly. The use of accordion gates in hallways is one good example.

Roof access—Problem visitors very commonly find their way onto a school's roof, where they engage in undesirable activities. Do heating tanks, electrical fixtures, or other features serve as unintended ladders, making roofs accessible? Remedies include removing the ladders or blocking the roof access point with nontraversable walls or fencing.

Safe materials—A design may use hazardous materials, such as concrete play areas or unforgiving climbing structures. Remedies include use of soft-impact materials and removal or repair of structures that can catch clothes, scrape skin, or otherwise injure.

Signs—Are the rules clear? Do students know that certain areas are off limits? Do they grasp that the grassy area is still school property, and that smoking is not allowed? Signs can help remedy these situations.

Sprawl—Many communities, as well as campuses, suffer from sprawl. When buildings are spread over a large area, they are much more difficult to monitor. Intruders can slip onto campus from multiple directions, and they can hide between buildings. The greater the number of buildings, the more entrances must be secured and/or monitored, and the more difficult school security becomes. Remedies include enclosing the campus to obligate entry through only one monitored gateway; installing more windows, mirrors, or cameras around campus; deploying campus patrols; or linking most buildings to restrict access to, from, and between them.

Traffic control—Does the movement of vehicles, bicycles, and pedestrians lead to risks or conflicts? Typical problems, which intensify during release and arrival times, include parking-lot chaos, unmarked crossings, and obscured crossings. Remedies may include changing traffic-flow patterns, moving pickup and dropoff locations, installing traffic-control devices, or installing mirrors.

Water fountains—Are water fountains frequently clogged or damaged? Are they placed in functional locations? Are they hidden from natural surveillance? Remedies include more protective designs or more open locations.

Windows—Do windows allow for natural surveillance? They may be installed too high for this purpose, covered with closed curtains, or glazed to obscure vision. Remedies may include installing, moving, uncovering, or reglazing windows. If breakage is a problem, options include security film, protective mesh covering, plastic windows, and alarmed windows.

Zones—Could this area be better managed if it were broken into zones? Sometimes an area is just too large to supervise. For example, allowing cars to park on all four sides of a building can pose this problem. Remedies include closing off sections of the school or campus, obliging all drivers to park in one lot, or using accordion gates to close off certain hallways so that basketball fans don't have the run of the school instead of just the gym.

Conducting the School-Site Evaluation

Evaluation of the school site begins with a close look at the environment in which it is placed. Typically, neighborhood and community problems spill over directly into the school setting. Conditions noted during the evaluation of the community will give school officials helpful clues as they seek ways to make both the school and the neighborhood safer for their students.

Who should conduct the assessment? A team, including an administrator, a teacher, a student, a custodian, and/or a school resource officer, can bring a broad perspective and diverse information to this process. Use of such a team is highly recommended.

Circling In

Begin the CPTED assessment process by working slowly around the outside of the site while taking notes on the forms provided, starting as far as four blocks away from the site and circling in. If the surrounding neighborhood is relatively impoverished and/or disorganized, there's a greater likelihood that the school experiences a high level of social disorder (Gottfredson 1997).

These neighborhood conditions may indicate that student safety en route to school needs to be a consideration. Safe areas where students can study on campus after school should assume greater urgency if students are unlikely to find an adequate workspace at home.

Other ways the school could reach out to the community—extending an umbrella of safety and order into the neighborhood—would be to institute adult literacy classes or family-support centers at the school.

These are but a few of the problems and potential solutions that careful assessment of the school's immediate community setting can indicate.

Some suggested questions to pose in evaluating the surrounding neighborhood and community are provided below.

- **Is the neighborhood a positive, negative, or neutral factor?**

  - Is it riddled with crime so that it poses a menace from which students should be protected and sheltered? Or can it serve as a resource for field trips and mentors?

Parents and Schools Succeeding in Providing Organized Routes to Travel (PASSPORT)

In the Visalia (California) Unified School District, Visalia Police, parents, and community-based organizations worked together to establish the PASSPORT program in response to concerns about safety for children walking to school through unsafe streets. Volunteers wear identification badges and commit themselves to watching certain routes during high-risk hours.

Contact: Ralph Lomeli, Safe Schools Coordinator, Visalia Unified School District, 315 East Acequia, Visalia, CA 93291; 209-730-7579.

- Chain stores and corporations often have grant programs available to local schools that are worth pursuing, and many businesses would help with fundraising if asked (for example, with cash donations, collection jars on the counter, or donated goods such as food for bake sales or contributed services to offer through a raffle).

- Apprenticeships, mentorships, and on-the-job training opportunities can be win-win arrangements, helping small businesses survive while providing job skills and valuable experience for students.

- Museums, exhibits, theaters, or recreation centers can provide enriching opportunities for student field trips. A show may be too expensive for most students, but the rehearsals might be open to a "practice" audience.

- Supportive neighbors can provide safe havens (such as Block Homes) for children traveling to or from school, or they might volunteer, if asked, to serve as tutors or to share their expertise as guest speakers in the classroom. Some might be willing to serve as crossing guards or playground monitors. Neighbors from varied backgrounds can be invaluable resources for bilingual education.

- A large facility nearby may be an essential resource if a school evacuation becomes necessary. Establish a relationship with the owners; know how to reach them in an emergency.

Any activities that build bridges to the community can potentially create more resources from which the school can draw as it seeks to fulfill its mission and increase its level of safety. The more neighbors feel connected to the school, the more likely they will extend themselves to the school and its students. If neighbors know the principal, they're that much more likely to call him or her about suspicious activities observed on school grounds after hours. Currying favor and developing positive relations with school neighbors can provide invaluable natural surveillance.

- **Do students walk, ride buses, ride bicycles, or drive, or do parents drop them off at school?**

Students' primary mode of transport will determine some safety concerns. Bus drivers may need safety training, corners may require crossing guards, and dropoff locations may need careful planning to avoid traffic snarls.

- **How safely could eight-year-olds walk through that part of town to get to school? Would they encounter traffic hazards? Passed-out drunks? Gang turf? Drug dealers or prostitutes? Do students express fear about traveling to and from school? Are there abandoned buildings where squatters might**

Travel between home and school can be designed for safety or perilously neglected.

be living? Could a child be lured into one of those buildings unnoticed? Are buildings boarded up?

If the journey looks perilous, school officials might want to promote car pooling, encourage students to walk in groups, add bus service, or assign crossing guards. Civic groups, resident associations, Neighborhood Watch groups, or police might be approached about neighborhood revitalization and community policing.

- **Are there areas where kids hang out during or after school, litter, harass the neighbors, smoke cigarettes, or worse?**

Students may have to walk a gauntlet of delinquents and gang members to get home. Extending positive school influence into the neighborhood can turn attitudes around. Community-service initiatives (such as building renovations, street-cleaning efforts, litter patrols, and similar measures) can help empower neighborhood residents to reclaim ownership and territoriality over their turf.

- **What kinds of video games are served up at the local shops—let alone on campus? Do these games portray human beings as targets for violence or abuse? What posters, billboards, or marquees do children see on a daily basis? Do they stereotype people based on race, gender, religion, or other attributes?**

Do they promote alcohol or cigarette use? Do they glorify violence?

If the destructive messages that some students observe on a daily basis overwhelm school attempts at instilling positive values, the school, neighborhood, and/or community may have a serious problem. A campaign to reduce or eliminate such negative influences can be an important educational experience for students and may also improve neighborhood and school climates.

Site Boundaries

Upon approaching the school, observe how many options are available to would-be intruders for gaining access. Ideally, fencing restricts access to only selected entry points. Those entry points should be controllable and fully securable by the school. Where fencing is not practical, the fall-back position should be extra vigilance in securing the school buildings themselves.

To establish territoriality, the entry area should be clearly marked with signs telling visitors what is expected of them. In addition to making the rules clear, these signs make confrontations more comfortable for staff, who don't have to wonder whether illegitimate trespassers grasp that they are unwelcome. Signs sending visitors to the office should be accompanied by site maps and arrows. Without them, intruders will feel empowered to wander the campus while "looking for the office."

Beyond Site Boundaries

Natural surveillance should extend beyond the school grounds, considering the surrounding neighborhood as well. It's not unusual for sites just beyond the school grounds to serve as gathering spots for nonschool youth. The presence of a police/school-security officer, or merely the knowl-edge that the gathering spots are under the gaze of school staff, can often convince a problematic group to move elsewhere.

Students are often at high risk of victimization after they leave school grounds. Recruiting neighboring businesses to keep lights on, or to stand sentry on the street, can make a huge difference in student safety.

Lighting

An afterdark site visit is essential to evaluate the adequacy of school lighting. School districts have been moving in the direction of darkened campuses for a number of years now, though some still promote full lighting. Both approaches have had some success. After schools in Oregon, Florida, California, and elsewhere went to blacked-out campuses over the past decade, they saw a significant drop in electricity bills as well as vandalism. There are two drawbacks: the schools may not be perceived as community resources during those dark hours, and conceivably illicit behavior could more easily go undetected on unlighted school grounds.

Advantages to lighted campuses include improved surveillance of the site from neighboring properties, passers-by, or patrol cars; maximized use of public facilities; and a stronger bond with the surrounding neighborhood. Legitimate activities on the school site can help discourage misuse; adult learners in attendance can provide positive role models for those younger and less experienced.

Partial lighting can be problematic: if the entry is brightly lit, but a nearby area is not, the human eye will adjust to the bright spot, causing the nearby shadowed area to become impenetrably black. This means it's a great place to hide, either to plan an assault on others visible in the brightly lit area or to commit other kinds of crimes. Watch for uneven lighting, including pockets of shadow created by shrubs, fencing, or dumpsters. These obstacles can provide hiding places in broad daylight, too. Trimming shrubs to no more than a few feet in height, lopping off tree limbs below six feet in height, and removing alternate slats from solid wood fences are easy solutions.

A related concern is excessive lighting. Massive security lights may annoy neighbors. They can also cause counterproductive glare, in which case neighbors can't see the campus, can't observe suspicious activity, and are thus less likely to call the police when they should. Thoughtful shielding can remedy this problem. Yet another concern to think about is unbalanced lighting. If the interior is brightly lit, while the exterior is dark, the occupants become overexposed. Intruders looking through the windows can see them, but the occupants can't see the intruders.

One reasonable approach is to go with darkened campuses but maintain the capacity for flexible scheduling. If someone wants to offer a night class at the school, it shouldn't be derailed because it would be after the scheduled blackout hour; nor should it be conducted with inadequate lighting inside or out. In addition, motion-response lights can be installed in chronically troubled locations where alert neighbors could be relied on to notice the light and respond appropriately.

Traffic, Crime, Dropoff Areas and Parking Lots

Are there traffic-calming devices on or near campus? Examples would include stop lights, blinking yellow lights, school-crossing markings, speed bumps, roundabouts (a cement circle or planter constructed in the middle of an intersection, forcing cars to slow down and drive around the obstruc-

Parking, Growth, and Entry Points

Schools, communities, and traffic patterns change over time. Small parking lots near the main entry may be outgrown, and additional parking may spring up in unanticipated locations, based solely on availability. In some cases these changes will have a ripple effect, as drivers now seek the most convenient access point from the new parking area to the school. The latter may be at quite a distance from the official main entry or office.

As this new development spirals out of control, the back door and/or breezeways may become the functional equivalent of the front of the school. When this happens, access control and natural surveillance usually deteriorate or disappear entirely. Behavioral modification may be attempted, such as discouraging students from opening the secure backdoors when people knock, or insisting that students circle the building and enter at the front. Even though the purpose of these measures is to protect those students already inside the school, they may expose the students trying to enter to a greater personal risk, and they are generally a poor fix for a dysfunctional layout.

From a preventive point of view, new parking or vehicle driveways should be planned with the bigger picture in mind, either routing all traffic to the intended entry or adding a guardian at the new point of entry. This new guardian might be a rebuilt front office at the new location, a secondary office at the new location, posting of staff, or other variations on this theme.

tion), or "woonerfs" (originally a Dutch design in which an area allows cars access but contains sufficient obstacles to oblige them to drive slowly). Sharp turns can slow traffic, but be wary of impatient drivers cutting corners. Best-case scenarios would place safety islands between opposing traffic lanes, bike lanes, and sidewalks. Bike lanes should parallel vehicle lanes and sidewalks to avoid any surprise conflicts; transportation paths should be predictable and safe.

One of the most common conflicts surfaces at pickup and dropoff times, when small children dash between large cars and buses, when older children recklessly peel out of parking lots, or parents rush to deliver their children to school on time. Pay attention to the actual traffic flow and how to control it. Must cars back out of parking spaces? Most parking-lot accidents involve backing up or out. Driving forward offers better visibility. Can fencing control the points at which children dash across traffic lanes? Sometimes an area needs to be redesigned to accommodate unforeseen foot-traffic patterns.

Parking lots can be hard to control if they're overly spread out. If lots are scattered throughout the property, they will be that much more difficult to patrol. Zoned lots, on the other hand, can force drivers to park closer together, providing enhanced mutual security through natural surveillance. Data indicate parking lots were the sites for 10.5 percent of all school-associated violent deaths, on or off campus, between 1992 and 1994 (Kachur, Stennies, Powell, and others 1996). A review of National School Safety Center files by the senior author found that between 1992 and 1998 parking lots were the most common outdoor, on-campus sites of school homicides.

Zoned lots use mechanical barriers to select which parking-lot sections will be available at particular times of day. By keeping parked vehicles in one controlled area, they will be easier to oversee using fewer staff.

The view of the parking lot from the main office is an important design consideration.

Vehicles that show up in the off-limits area become that much more apparent, and staff can respond appropriately.

For those high-school students who drive their cars to school, a requirement that they obtain and pay for parking permits has several advantages in addition to the income from fees, which help to cover school expenses. Permit-revocation can serve as leverage to encourage courteous driving, and the record-keeping for permits makes it easier to determine who owns which car.

In the most extreme situations, parking lots may require continual monitoring in the form of a parking-lot attendant, as well as entrance and exit control gates. These can be enhanced with wrong-way puncture devices that make entering through the exit, or exiting through the entrance, physically impossible.

A related concern is the environment inside the school bus, as it transports students to and from school. If the bus is an environment beyond the driver's control, human or electronic monitoring can help. Consider encouraging parents, police, or volunteers to ride the bus as well. Parents of problem kids might be required to escort their children to school until their behavior is brought under control.

Bike Paths

Urban bike paths may generate some controversy, usually among property owners who fear that paths will lead to crime. Studies of rails-to-trails paths, particularly in Seattle, suggest that paths do not generate crime and in fact they raise property values. The senior author's review of National School Safety Center files found no mention of bike paths in any school homicides nationwide. Isolation and a lack of surveillance are key factors in path safety, just as these factors heighten the risk of victimization anywhere else.

Crimes near paths in Lane County, Oregon, have almost always taken place in hidden areas adjacent to the path, rather than the path itself. This risk can be mitigated by clearing thick brush near the paths and encouraging people not to travel alone (a good precaution regardless of location).

Another major issue regarding paths is whether they undermine access control for the school. At first glance, paths may appear to do so, but frequently the access already existed as an undeveloped open space, such as an abandoned lot, rail line, or riverbank. In those cases, the access was already undermined—intruders could enter at will. The distinction a bike path brings is that now legitimate users are also present, and usually they constitute the majority. As a result, this legitimate presence improves security throughout the area by mitigating the isolation and lack of territoriality that existed before. Legitimate users of the area can discover suspicious activity, discourage it, report it, or intervene directly. In such a scenario, the path makes the location safer by bringing in natural surveillance.

A further consideration with bike paths is the level of risk students can avoid by using the new path. If the path is well designed, it will be sufficiently removed from urban congestion to avoid traffic hazards, but it will stay close enough to potential allies to maintain safety. If neighboring homes have a view of the path, for example, users will be safer because somebody can see their distress and call for help. If the alternative is to force the student to ride on a congested road, the risk of vehicle-versus-bicycle accidents will far exceed the likelihood of a problem on a well-planned, off-road trail.

Fencing

What type of fencing is used? Solid walls and certain types of fencing block natural surveillance, thereby reducing security. Fences and walls also provide attractive canvases for graffiti, which means higher maintenance costs for the school. Graffiti must be removed as quickly as possible (preferably within 24 hours) to send a clear message to gangs that they are not welcome. In some cases, special coatings can be applied to surfaces, making it easier to remove

The "dead wall" on the left blocks natural surveillance; the mesh fence on the right does not.

graffiti with a special cleanser. This isn't always the most cost-effective approach; if the graffiti is infrequent you may be better off simply painting over it.

Wrought-iron fencing is the best choice because it provides no significant surface for graffiti, is extremely vandal resistant, and requires minimal maintenance. Although it is expensive, wrought-iron fencing is extremely durable. A common practical compromise is chain-link fencing. Drawbacks to chain-link are its vulnerability to cutting, ramming, or climbing, and its dreary institutional appearance. Wrought-iron fencing, on the other hand, enhances a school's climate, reinforcing an image of a solid, enduring institution. Chain-link, at its worst, can reinforce a storage yard, industrial image.

School Grounds

Study the grounds on each side of the school building—north, south, east, and west—separately and ask the following questions:

• Which hazards are present?

• What obstacles are there to clear vision? Does the landscaping create blind spots?

• Are playground areas safe to fall, run, or play on? Are there hard surfaces or sharp edges? Are there protruding objects that might injure students or snag clothing, or which could possibly cause other injuries?

• Are water fountains and bathrooms accessible?

• Are there shaded areas for hot-weather activities?

• Are weeds and pests controlled with toxic chemicals that pose a health hazard to students? On the other hand, do uncontrolled weeds and pests pose hazards, such as tripping, or stumbling into a bees' nest?

• What about public events, such as ball games? Where do visitors park? Can they find their way around? Can you control access to the field?

• What kinds of activities occur on the grounds? Which of these are desirable, and which are not? Which are school functions?

Parents predictably will park along this fence line while attending athletic events.

• Does a rough crowd tend to hang out? How could you change the environment to diminish its appeal to this group? Would they appreciate unappealing lighting or piped-in music?

Sprawl and Access Control

Does the school lean toward a sprawling campus or a fortress-like design? A sprawling campus, just like a sprawling city, is harder to patrol. Such campuses are highly permeable; visitors may be able to slip between buildings throughout the campus. Security, in this case, could be a daunting challenge. Sprawling campuses can be made safer by taking the following steps:

1. Close the gaps. Link all the buildings with wrought-iron fencing and gates. Done effectively, this forces visitors to enter through selected entry points, where they can at least be observed (and in some cases interviewed), passed through a metal detector, or even frisked depending on the level of risk and suspicion. By using wrought-iron instead of solid walls, the school retains natural surveillance. Children in trouble outside the walls can still be seen, heard, and rescued.

Another option is to construct substantial, solid walls, usually of a design and material compatible with existing structures.

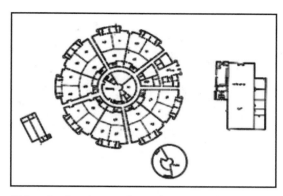

This school is designed as a fortress. A lack of windows means no surveillance of the surroundings and no natural light for students.

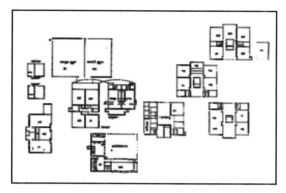

This campus suffers from sprawl; access control is impractical.

The walls should be insurmountable and should contain windows. The windows can use wrought-iron bars instead of glass.

Breezeways can be converted into enclosed hallways, ideally with pitched roofs replacing flat designs. The flat designs make roof trespass easy and enticing, and they tend to leak, requiring more frequent maintenance. A pitched-metal roof is less conducive to intruders and less maintenance-intensive. In some cases the inner wall of the hall can be left open to the new, fully enclosed, inner courtyard, primarily as a cost-saving feature. The newly converted hallway can also be designed with a generous width to accommodate a wider distribution of lockers, mitigating density and conflict problems between classes. One school reportedly has used glassed-in breezeways to some advantage by integrating passive solar heating into their plans as well.

A very important issue that arises with this type of redesign is the potential for conflicts with building safety codes. Attaching buildings with solid walls or even fencing can be construed as creating one large building, and this may engender some fire risks that must be addressed. This is not an insurmountable problem. Often it can be resolved by adding a sprinkler system, or by installing firewalls in certain locations, to restrict a fire's ability to move quickly from one wing to another. As one architect pointed out, the reduced insurance costs that come with the installation of sprinkler systems should more than cover the costs of the retrofitting!

(As an example, see Case Study: St. Helena Elementary in the next chapter.)

2. Make each building a secure facility in and of itself. When facilities are scattered throughout the community or the campus is widely accessible because of excessive sprawl, site-containment is not a realistic option. Security under those circumstances may need to focus on each building separately, with each entry area designed for maximum natural surveillance and access control. Ideally these entries will be staffed, with the degree of screening commensurate with the perception of risk. Access-control devices, such as swipe cards, may be necessary as well.

Building-to-building communication devices will be unavoidable necessities. In addition, if circumstances dictate that fewer CPTED measures can be applied, the greater will be the demand for human surveillance to compensate. One result is that teachers will have to spend that much more time on security patrol.

The portable buildings on the left obliged the main building to leave backdoors unlocked, eliminating access control.

Wrought-iron fencing reestablishes access control without compromising natural surveillance.

Fortresses

Fortress-like school buildings usually have an advantage over sprawling campuses—there's only one building to control, and once students are inside the risk is contained. Their primary disadvantage is akin to what is seen in gated communities: it may be safe on the inside, but it becomes that much more dangerous once you leave. The barricading wall that keeps people secure on the inside also prevents staff members from seeing vulnerable students should they be accosted outside the walls. An important fact to remember: the risk level for school-related victimization generally doubles once students leave the building!

Those solid walls will also hide afterhours intruders from vigilant neighbors. This risk can be reduced by replacing the walls with a less obstructing style (such as trading solid walls for wrought-iron fencing), and by taking care in the location and installation of windows.

Avoid placing solid or "dead" walls along the outer skin of the building. The hidden areas that can result may become magnets for illicit activities. Dark or hidden alcoves, commonly found at loading docks or sheltered entry areas, are especially attractive to trespassers—or troubled students—looking for a spot to engage in destructive behavior.

Loading docks, garbage areas, utility or storage boxes, window sills, and many architectural features also frequently offer easy roof access to intruders. Be careful to control access to these areas.

A fortress-like design may be great up to a point, but there is a limit. One large school building may be just as unwieldy to monitor, supervise, and care for as is a sprawling campus. One school police officer, referring to such a school, reported that there were at least 60 doors in the school building to monitor.

Hiding Places

Every blind corner is a potential hazard. Make it easy for people to see what's coming. If the blind corner is unavoidable, reduce the risk where possible by installing windows, mounting convex mirrors strategically close to the corners, or moving the walkway at least a few feet away from the building. This adds a margin of safety as pedestrians round the bend, so that they can avoid being taken by surprise.

Teacher presence has been shown to be a major school-safety factor. Building in natural surveillance is a great way to make the most efficient use of these staff resources.

Unnecessary visual barriers create a hiding place for illicit activities.

Video Cameras

Some school officials believe security can be enhanced by installing surveillance cameras. In hidden areas, such as fire stairwells, they may be the only realistic option. Unfortunately, cameras aren't a significant crime deterrent. They can, however, be invaluable in identifying culprits after the fact. One source suggests that tapes can serve as teaching tools if students are allowed to view the videotapes and learn from their own misbehavior (Curwin and Mendler 1997).

Some institutions install multiple monitors in a back room and pay security officers to watch them. This expectation is probably unrealistic. Studies conducted two decades ago demonstrated that twenty minutes was about the limit for attentive viewing, even with motivated watchers (Green 1999).

Camera technology continues to change, and quality continues to improve. Pan-tilt cameras historically have tended to require high maintenance, and Murphy's Law frequently seems to keep them from capturing critical events. Fiber-optic cabling allows the greatest distance between camera and receivers in a hard-wired system; wireless models are dependent on repeaters to relay signals about every 1,500 feet. As wireless technology has improved, this option has become increasingly attractive. Installation professionals can be consulted about what

Impact of Adult Presence

"In a survey of more than 100 students, teachers, and administrators at five midwestern high schools, Ron A. Astor, professor of social work and education, University of Michigan, found that, of the 166 reported acts of school violence, all occurred in locations where few or no adults—especially teachers—were present. About 40% of the incidents took place in hallways between class periods, while another 20% occurred in cafeterias during lunchtime. Other dangerous areas included gyms, locker rooms, auditoriums, and parking lots, especially right before or after the school day..."

"While teachers in the study indicated a sense of ownership and responsibility for the space within their classrooms, many were reluctant to extend that feeling to areas of 'undefined public space,' which accounts for about a third of all school space... the students in the study said that 'unowned' public places must be 'personally reclaimed' by adults who have authority, know students personally, and know what procedure to follow when conflict arises in those locations...."

"'By far, the most effective violence intervention described by students, teachers, and administrators was the physical presence of teachers who are willing to intervene, coupled with a clear, consistent administrative policy on violence,' Astor explains."

SOURCE: *USA Today*, December 1996, v.125, n. 2619 p.13 (1)

works best in a given location. Signs can be posted warning that video surveillance *may* be used if vandalism or other criminal activity becomes a problem. The signs themselves may be effective deterrents. At the same time, avoid implying that security services are in place if they are not. If someone is victimized, they might have a legal

This video surveillance image of Kip Kinkel approaching Thurston High School illustrates the severe limitations of surveillance cameras as security devices. Kinkel is not identifiable in this image, nor is it obvious that he poses a threat.

days pass before evidence is erased or taped over.

Common concerns with cameras: Some of the most common complaints about cameras are that (1) they get vandalized or stolen, and (2) they do not capture adequate pictures. Bear these considerations in mind while choosing camera locations, and insist on field testing equipment before making a final purchase.

Final points about cameras: The price of a good one could equal the cost of installing one or more windows or a panic-button alarm, adding convex mirrors to all major hallway intersections, and/or purchasing numerous violence-prevention curricula. The camera can document trouble-makers, and the windows and mirrors can help to spot and deter them; the social ecology of the school, on the other hand, is more likely to prevent them!

argument that they reasonably assumed a higher level of security than actually existed. For this reason, signs saying "surveillance cameras in use" should only be installed when this is accurate.

Schools have had good success with cameras temporarily installed at trouble spots to identify culprits and confront them later. With adequate attic space, wires can be strung with reasonable ease, but where this is not the case a wireless model is far preferable.

Portable systems offer an economical alternative, giving districts the flexibility of moving cameras to various locations as needed. Portable cameras also give the school the option of buying fewer systems of higher quality rather than wholesale lots of cheaper cameras to accommodate a large number of locations on a permanent basis.

Each camera will also require a slow-speed recording device, and personnel will be obliged to change the tapes daily. At least seven tapes should be on hand, one for each day of the week. In this manner at least six

Territoriality

As mentioned earlier, territoriality is the third key component of CPTED, along with natural surveillance and natural access control. Establishing territoriality involves sending a clear message to others that says, "We're in charge here." In schools, it also helps reinforce a message among students and staff that says, "We belong here and this is our school."

In conducting a CPTED assessment, watch for positive and negative territorial messages. The most common negative messages are in the form of graffiti. Whether it's gang graffiti on the gym walls or racist graffiti in a bathroom stall, the effect can still be demoralizing and fear-inducing.

The Electronic Surveillance Paradox

Closed Circuit Television (CCTV), and to some degree the entire concept of surveillance, can be looked at as logical extensions of the thinking behind the Panopticon prison model of the nineteenth century. This approach suggested building a facility in which all residents were under constant natural surveillance without necessarily being able to see the viewer.

The concept is a powerful one, with great potential for both use and abuse, particularly in a nonprison setting.

CCTV has become widely popular in a variety of locations, ranging from prisons to public squares. It has been remarkably effective for influencing traffic behavior in Australia and Canada, reducing speeding vehicles in one location five-fold, with a subsequent drop in injuries from 40,000 to 15,000 annually, and with fatalities dropping from 1,000 to fewer than 250.

This electronic surveillance is purely objective, with no decisions made based on protected class or other factors vulnerable to prejudice. Some suggest that one result of this objectivity should be a rise in enforcement against previously underpoliced groups, and it can thus be an equalizer that sensitizes privileged groups to the same level of accountability imposed on more conventionally targeted classes.

But CCTV also has an Orwellian side. The omnipresence of Big Brother can undermine the quality of freedom in a society, throwing a chill into politically unpopular or diverse activities that can be scrutinized and ostensibly punished. Whether or not authorities abuse this technology, as long as the perception suggests that this could happen, democratic freedoms may be undermined.

For these reasons, the use of CCTV should be thoughtfully weighed and carefully monitored. As authors Clive Norris and Gary Armstrong observed, "the only criterion which distinguishes a modern traffic control system from the apparatus of political control is democratic accountability" (Norris and Armstong 1999).

Positive countermeasures can include painting over or removing graffiti. Going one step further, schools can display artwork or banners that send constructive territorial messages, such as "Pursuing truth in the company of friends."

School uniforms have emerged as a very powerful tool for establishing territoriality. A 1997 study found that 41 percent of elementary school principals were in favor of school uniforms (see National Association of Elementary School Principals 1997). Schools ranging from Long Beach, California, to Springfield, Oregon, and eastward across the country, report that student misbehavior decreased once uniforms became mandatory.

Many side benefits can accrue from school uniforms: intruders will stand out like sore thumbs; families are relieved of the financial burden of buying "fashionable" wardrobes for their children; and gang attire becomes a moot point. Furthermore, when young people are accused of misbehavior in the neighborhood, uniforms or the lack of them will help identify perpetrators, and possibly protect a student and, by association, the school from being falsely accused!

The Entry Area

The main office should be the primary gate-keeper for the school, with its staff monitoring all who enter the building. Everyone approaching at the primary entry point should pass the main office and be seen by the staff. The office should use glass extensively, and office staff should have unobstructed views in all directions.

The main office should also have a clear view of the grounds whenever possible, especially the main entry area, main drive, bus loading zone, and main parking area. If staff in the office can also observe the main play-

A deadwall blocks natural surveillance of approaching visitors at this site.

This office sits far back from the entry doors. An architectural feature partially blocks the view.

Surveillance can be restored by installing windows

This office is located directly inside the main doors, but the view is blocked by an art display on the windows.

ground, so much the better. At the very least, making this a reality in most schools will involve putting windows in a few dead walls. At worst, it will involve extensive renovation and new construction, resulting in an office space that extends out the front of the building.

Visitors should be visually drawn to this one entry, and indicators should clearly communicate the steps they will have to take to enter the building. For example, arrows, maps, and multilingual signs might inform them that they will be buzzed in electronically if they will check in at the external sliding office window adjacent to the front doors. At the window, visitors will be asked to state their business and answer any relevant questions, and then they will be given a visitor's tag. A large, prominently displayed, conveniently located sign should

share important information, display a map, and guide visitors to appropriate locations.

Metal Detectors

A significant number of schools, especially in major urban areas, have determined that the number of weapons showing up on campus warrants installing metal detectors. Fifteen percent of schools surveyed nationally in 1994 were already using metal detectors; 11-13 percent reported using them in 1998, though with varying degrees of rigor.

Metal detectors appear regularly on lists of security recommendations, and under certain circumstances they may be wise investments. To be effective, however, there must not be *any* other way to enter the school, such as through another unlocked door or

Security Vestibules

For schools experiencing chronic problems with weapons violations, metal detectors may become necessary investments. The cost of the scanning portal, wands, and x-ray machine, coupled with the considerable expense of staffing the equipment, may make it reasonable to consider a fully contained security vestibule as an alternative.

Security vestibules are more commonly associated with financial and commercial buildings. They provide a high-security, fully contained entry vestibule that a visitor must pass through to reach the facility. If the metal detector is triggered, the second door will not open, and the visitor has no alternative but to turn around and leave. There are no guards present to put at risk, to argue with, or to require salaries.

A built-in camera and intercom allow the central office or a security officer to communicate with visitors from a safe distance and to make judgment calls about overriding the detector and allowing access. Visitors can also be instructed to open their coats and backpacks and display contents to the camera—all at a safe distance from school staff. People exiting the building also pass through a vestibule designed to make entry through the exit impossible. Additional features may include:

• weight-sensing floor mats that prevent more than one person from entering

• emergency backup power

• fire and ADA compliance

• "trapping" capability if a facility wants to ensnare a person leaving through the vestibule

• various levels of bullet-resistant glass

There are some difficulties with incorporating such a vestibule into a school:

• Vestibules will allow a customer flow rate of 3-5 seconds per person; the sheer volume and intensity of pedestrian traffic in a school may pose a potential traffic-jam situation.

• Fire and life safety-code issues may need to be addressed.

• Emergency access for firefighters or police needs to be built into the system (emergency override buttons and wireless remote controls are available).

• The vestibules can be quite expensive, ranging from $48,500 to $81,700 per vestibule in one recent quote.

None of these problems is insurmountable, and even the steep cost may be justifiable in comparison to the ongoing costs of staffing conventional entries.

With a large, sprawling facility, vestibules might be needed in multiple locations. Additional, conventional entries and exits would still be options for the schools to use as they saw fit. The advantage would be a facility that still allows reasonable access from each side, while still screening out weapons.

For more information, one manufacturer to contact is Diebold, P.O. Box 3077, Dept. 9-79, North Canton, Ohio 44720-8077.

window, and the equipment must be supervised by staff prepared to disarm intruders. These requirements ratchet up the costs of using metal detectors in schools.

Metal detectors do have their share of critics. In an *Education Digest* article in September 1994, Del Stover expressed concern that high schools risk becoming indistinguishable from high-tech prisons if they overinvest in security devices. Writing in *Scholastic Update* that same year, Karen N. Peart took a look at Wingate High School in the Crown Heights section of Brooklyn, New York, which installed metal detectors in 1990 after being rated one of the city's five most dangerous high schools. She quoted one student as saying, "It makes me feel safer," while others complained that the school felt too prison-like.

Wingate's use of detectors encountered some implementation and technical problems. Scanning of students was conducted intermittently, on a random basis, because scanning all students required too much time. Students reported that they could undermine the effectiveness of the metal detectors by hiding weapons behind belt buckles. According to Peart, the school's principal, Richard Organisciak, felt that the money might have been better spent on new books and peer-mediation training.

Organisciak's sentiments are understandable. Nevertheless, approximately 973,000 students brought handguns to school in the past year on one or more occasions, and that cannot be ignored. The fact that one is safer from victimization by gun violence in prisons than in our public schools should be alarming. Metal detectors may be controversial, but they should undoubtedly be considered, along with all other options, in choosing the right mix of safety measures for a particular school.

Making schools safer and violence-free requires a comprehensive approach. When schools are at a severe level of risk, it may be necessary to consider options that previously had been considered unpalatable.

Office Design and Safety Concerns

Although it may not have always been the case, the role of the office as school guardian is now of primary importance. The office should be located and designed in a manner that reinforces this critical role. The strategic function of the school office in advancing safety and security can be accomplished by emphasizing natural surveillance, natural access control, and territoriality in office placement and design.

Basic design considerations. School office design and operational issues are critical to overall school safety and security: good interschool communication devices, working PA systems, and annunciators indicating when exterior doors are opened are all examples of basic strategies. Confidential materials need to be filed securely; confiscated drugs or weapons, lost and found items, and teachers' mailboxes need similar protection. If these secure spaces aren't planned for, the result may be a congested, inefficient workspace. Similarly, room for copy machines, fax machines, printers, and telephone equipment boxes is necessary to permit staff members' freedom of movement.

Receptionists, as the first line of defense, need the basic protection of a counter, topped in extreme cases with a protective plexiglass shield. Seating should be available to de-escalate confrontations—it's harder to be aggressive or attack from a seated position.

Office staff members should also have a safe haven to which they can retreat if threatened, usually another room with a lockable door and a working phone. The principal's office should always have two exits, even if one is a window. The nurse's office needs easy accessibility for stretchers and access to an ambulance without parading a sick or injured student through the halls.

And what about students sent to the principal for disciplinary reasons? Where are they to be placed and how are they accommodated? Does the child sent to the office for disruptive behavior share space with another child waiting to be picked up for a dental appointment?

Role of the office in access control. The office needs to be placed at the main entrance. Under the best of circumstances it should be designed to be fully capable of maintaining absolute control over school access as necessary. Very commonly, schools fall short of this level of security, by as much as six out of seven levels (see illustrations in figures 4-1 to 4-7) on the following scale developed by Schneider:

Level 1. At the lowest security level, the office is hidden deep within the building, allowing no significant surveillance, territoriality, or access control.

Level 2. The office is located along a main corridor, but has no access control, and very limited natural surveillance into the hall.

Level 3. The office extends into the hallway, allowing surveillance up and down the hall.

Level 4. The office also incorporates surveillance to the outside of the building.

Level 5. The entry is adjacent to the office, giving greatly improved surveillance capability to the office staff.

Level 6. All building entry doors are now secured, obliging visitors to enter adjacent to the main entrance. This brings the school to an optimum level of natural surveillance, but access control is still negligible.

Level 7. Only at the seventh level is natural surveillance matched with true access control. Visitors must pass through an entry vestibule, check in at the office, and be buzzed electronically through a second set of doors. Metal detectors can be incorporated into the first set of doors, alerting school staff when more careful examination of visitors is warranted.

Hallways

In a recent midwestern study, school hallways were identified as the location for 40 percent of school conflicts (*Caught in the Crossfire: A Report on Gun Violence in Our Schools* 1990). This study identified hallways as the site of one out of four shootings in schools—the most common indoor location for such tragedies. Our examination of National School Safety Center case files corroborates this finding.

A more recent report identifies hallways as the location for 8.6 percent of all school-associated violent deaths (indoors, outdoors, on or off campus) between 1992 and 1994 (Kachur, Stennies, and Powell and others 1996).

Hallways are generally long and have dead walls, which block off all natural surveillance. Their usage patterns tend to fluctuate—with intensive use followed generally by 45 minutes or so of nonuse; this pattern repeats throughout the school day.

An empty hallway can be a foreboding space. Metal lockers, hard tile floors, and even painted-over acoustic ceiling tiles produce an echo chamber with an ambiance similar to that of a multistory parking garage.

Hallways are common locations for fire alarms, which in turn are popular targets for some troublesome students. In Jonesboro, Arkansas, two boys used such an alarm to lure students and school staff members outdoors and shoot them in April 1998. Three sixth-graders plotted a similar attack in St. Charles, Missouri, the next month but didn't

Figure 4-1

Level 1:
Lowest Security Level

Office is hidden inside building.

No surveillance inside.

No access control.

Visitors who respond to signs directing them to office have permission to roam through entire building while seeking the office.

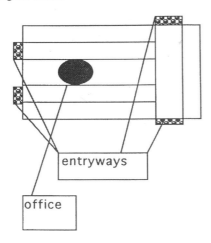

Figure 4-2

Level 2:
Office Is Located
Along Main Hallway

Office is located along main hallway.

Minimal surveillance inside main hallway limited to area directly adjacent to office.

Multiple entries.

Still no access control.

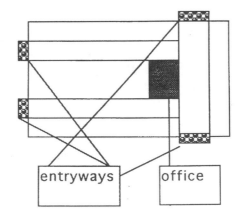

Figure 4-3

Level 3:
Office Extends into
Main Hallway

Office extends into main hallway.

Windows are installed on all sides

Improved surveillance up and down main hallway, including main entrees, but no surveillance up and down additional hallways.

Still no access control.

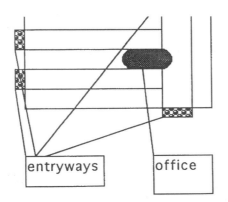

Figure 4-4

Level 4:
Office Extends into Main Hallway
and Includes View to Outside

Office extends into main hallway and includes view to outside.

Improved surveillance inside and out.

Office staff potentially have direct views into all 3 hallways.

Still no access control—staff can see some visitors after they enter, but can't prevent them from entering.

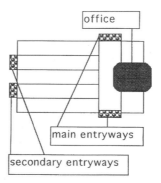

Figure 4-5

Level 5:
Entry Design Now Heightens Surveillance Capability

Entry design now heightens surveillance capability.

Visitors must now pass directly adjacent to the main office while entering or leaving. This strengthens territoriality and positions staff to intervene more directly with an unwelcome visitor.

Extended office design now allows surveillance up and down hallways, into main entry areas, and outside the main entry.

Access control is still lacking.

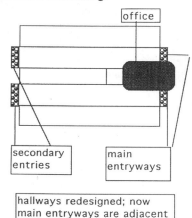

secondary entries

main entryways

hallways redesigned; now main entryways are adjacent to office

Figure 4-6

Level 6:
Multiple Entries Have Now Been Reduced

Multiple entries have now been reduced. Only one door is the main entry, two are fire exits, and one is the primary exit.

Surveillance is further improved.

Access control is still lacking.

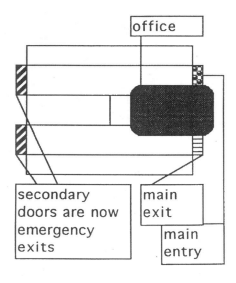

office

secondary doors are now emergency exits

main exit

main entry

Figure 4-7

Level 7:
The Main Entry Door Now Leads to a Double-Door Decompression Chamber/Vestibule

The main entry door now leads to a double-door decompression chamber/vestibule.

Visitor access is electronically controllable from the office; at any time, the office staff can electronically control the second set of doors, requiring visitors to check in at a sliding window before further access is allowed.

Emergency exits can be alarmed, and/or annunciators in office can indicate when doors are opened.

Metal detectors can be located inside the first set of double doors. If detectors are triggered, the second set of doors won't open until released by office staff. Pass-through windows into office allow visitors to empty pockets (similar to an airport).

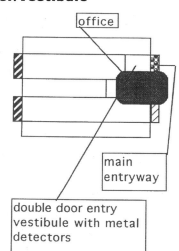

office

main entryway

double door entry vestibule with metal detectors

carry out the attack. Placing the fire alarms in a location that allows natural surveillance can cut down on the possibility they will be tampered with.

Murals on these walls include directional signs to help visitors or new students find their way.

All too often the hallway turns into a mosh pit of shoving, jostling, pestering, yelling, flirting, harassing, and bullying going on at once. Abutting lockers virtually guarantee student conflicts as one open door must crash into the neighboring locker or its owner. The chaotic atmosphere, a floor design that incorporates multiple escape routes, multiple visual obstacles (including classroom doors, locker doors, and students), overcrowding, and a nonterritorial climate all help establish a location that is particularly inviting for conflict and destructive behavior.

Some remedies to these common hallway problems include:

- **Schedule locker access.** If lockers were painted alternate colors, and only blue lockers could be opened during first, third, and fifth periods, while only red lockers could be opened during second, fourth, and sixth periods, conflicts would be reduced.

- **Stagger class times.** If ninth-grade classes ended at ten minutes after the hour, and tenth-grade classes ended at twenty minutes after the hour, hallway traffic would be drastically reduced.

- **Design new construction to allow more hall space**. The following design features are worth considering: recess lockers into niches out of the hall traffic; recess doorways out of the hall traffic; install lockers farther apart; muffle hallway noise; and improve visibility around blind corners with the use of rounded or "chamfered" corners and convex mirrors. At the same time, care should be taken not to create nooks in which perpetrators can hide their behavior from monitors.

- **Avoid "dead" wall designs.** Unused wall space should be given to adjacent teachers to use for displays. This usage increases a sense of ownership over that particular hall space; teachers and students are more inclined to check when they hear disruptive activity in the hall that may threaten their artwork.

- **Improve surveillance**. One-way mirrors and/or convex mirrors can give students the impression that teachers might be watching, and this knowledge may have a beneficial effect on their behavior, even if staff members aren't in a position to monitor the halls. Actual surveillance provided by trained adults is the ideal, of course. At the same time, a positive school climate can be undermined if grim security guards contribute to an oppressive or fearful atmosphere.

One option that seems effective has been to recruit students' parents to be a presence at schools. Principal Jacqueline Greenwood recruited fathers to serve this purpose at Arlington High School in Indianapolis in the late 1980s (Kipnis 1999). An Oakland, California, junior high school had success with hiring mothers and grandmothers, who substituted hugs and greetings for more conventional means of student control. Where admonishments were necessary, students were much more concerned about disappointing grandma than they were about distressing a security guard (Noguera 1995). The unfortunate drawback to any of these human or organizational approaches is the tremendous amount of energy required to maintain an adequate level of family and community involvement over a long period.

Restrooms

Restrooms can be dreaded campus locations. It is estimated that 22 percent of students are afraid to use school bathrooms because they are sites of frequent victimization. Once students go in there, no one can hear them being victimized. School bathrooms have long been havens for vandalism, cigarette smoking, drug use, shakedowns, and general havoc.

If a school could make only one change to bathrooms, it might consider eliminating double-door entries. Squeamishness about bathroom noises led to the creation of a commonly used, sound-muffling design. Unfortunately, double-door entries provide student victimizers on the inside with plenty

The stall with the greatest privacy has generated litter and graffitti while the other stalls have not.

Locking open the outer door creates a maze entry, discouraging misbehavior.

of warning when someone is coming, because they can hear the first door open and close before the second door moves. By changing to a maze design, schools can eliminate the early warning system, and make it easier for teachers to hear assaults on persons or property in progress.

A classic problem with bathrooms involves their locations. Frequently they are installed in hidden or obscure locations, further reducing natural surveillance. Ideally, bathrooms should be installed near natural surveillance points, such as the main school office.

Bathroom access is frequently a concern for afterschool sports events. A lack of facilities invites inappropriate use of the landscaping or other locations on the site; on the other hand, poorly sited facilities may invite visitors to have the run of the school to reach bathrooms. School restrooms often see their worst abuse from visitors, such as opposing teams. A location adjacent to the playing field is easier to supervise than facilities at a great distance or in a hidden location. The choice of materials and mounting hardware should be made with vandalism-resistance in mind.

Central Courtyard

Central courtyards are common features of many schools. If they are fully enclosed by the school building, security should not be a problem; in most cases, the fire code will require at least two or three emergency exits distant from each other. Many courtyards, however, are open on at least one side. Sometimes the central courtyard is a three-sided space at the main entrance, with multiple doorways leading in all directions, making access control extremely difficult.

As schools design courtyards, they should envision some worst-case scenarios. For example, how could they keep unwanted intruders out? At the same time, how can they be sure they haven't trapped students in a blind alley? The horror stories that administrators fear the most may never come about, but they can almost always count on problems with graffiti, skateboarding, or other chronic afterhours annoyances as possibilities within courtyards.

Illustrations A and B (on the following page) demonstrate two approaches to courtyard and office design. In illustration A, the office has retreated from the guardian position; access is wide open via the main entry area as well as the two hidden entrances. In illustration B, the office is more aggressively positioned. This exaggerated emphasis locates the office in a position that allows surveillance over as much of the site as possible. Offices that are flush with the building often pay for this position with restricted surveillance.

Flame Detectors

A New Tool for Smoking Enforcement

One technological innovation holds promise for deterring or intercepting bathroom smokers as soon as they light a match. The Stealth Smoking Enforcement System offers a variety of overt and covert devices that are actually triggered by the flame of a lighter or match within thirty feet of the detector.

The overt model looks like a smoke detector, and can be provided with a protective cage; the flame can trigger a conventional sound alarm or a recorded message. Covert models may look like sprinkler heads, deodorizers, or vents, and can also send a message to a central console, identifying the location of the incident. This allows school staff to actually intercept the offender at the scene. The sound alarm relies on culprits learning from experience, and leaves it at that.

The equipment comes in battery-operated, hard-wired, and wireless-remote versions. Costs range from $249 for a hardwired detector, plus $39 for a protective cage, to $2,399 for a "6 pack" wireless kit, which includes six detection devices and a receiver.

The manufacturer lists a number of satisfied customers, including the Chicago Transit Authority, Lucent Technologies, Levi Strauss, Brookfield Academy, and Palmyra Schools. For more information, contact: Voice Products, phone: 216-360-0433, fax: 216-360-9805, address: 23715 Mercantile Road #200, Cleveland, Ohio 44122. Email: vproducts@cyberdrive.net

Gymnasiums, Auditoriums, and Cafeterias

Large gathering areas can have very different purposes. Gymnasiums, for example, can function very effectively as sporting facilities, whereas their excessive reverberance

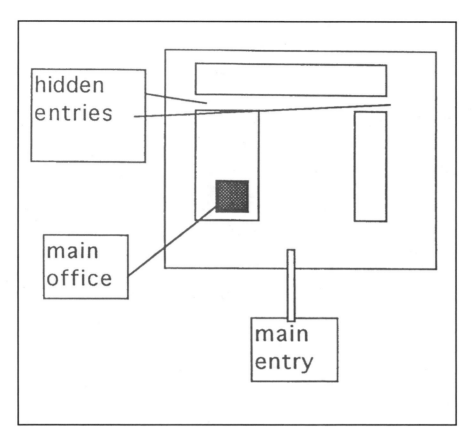

Illustration A:
The central courtyard is accessible via two hidden entries and a broad front entrance. The office is slightly withdrawn and cannot serve a gatekeeping function.

Illustration B: *The hidden entries are now equip0ped with fire doors, which can be unlocked as appropriate, and which are always accessible as fire exits. Visitors are now obligated to enter via the main entry, where the office has been extended into a more vigilant position. The broad front entrance is now controlled by a series of wrought-iron gates or fire doors. Visitors are funneled to the main entry, adjacent to the main office.*

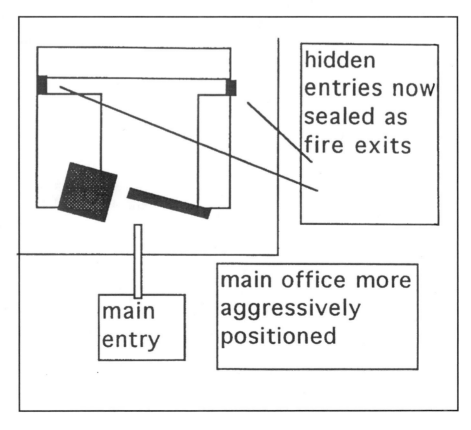

the locker room. Unfortunately, in many cases where such windows exist, the coaches cover them out of discomfort, or out of respect for student privacy. Nevertheless, just like anywhere else at school, an attentive adult is very effective at deterring misbehavior. If problems persist, student safety should take precedence over student privacy. Other options would include reducing locker height and redesigning locker-room layout(s) to make entrapment difficult.

would hardly suit a recital. Concert halls have very different acoustical needs.

Gymnasiums and auditoriums share one characteristic with cafeterias: large crowds move in and out at close to the same time. Watch for traffic-flow conflicts and design to avoid them. The home team can have a different door than is used by the visiting team, for example. Cafeteria conflicts can be controlled through scheduling, clear identification of one-way entry and exit doors, and effective monitoring by caring adults. Cafeterias also suffer from excess reverberance. Astor's study of midwestern high schools identified cafeterias as the site for one out of every five school-site conflicts ("Teachers' Presence May Deter Violence," December 1996).

Locker Rooms and Showers

Any place where a victim can be caught isolated or in a state of undress will be a temptation to offenders. Some schools have seen locker-room behavior deteriorate to the point where they have done away with showers, or even physical-education uniforms, to avoid the need for undressing and the risks inherent with such vulnerability.

A simpler adjustment would be to put a window in the coach's office looking into

Public Access and Afterhours Sports Events

A common oversight in site planning concerns bathroom access for the large crowds that turn out for sports events after hours or on the weekends. Bathroom access will be a critical issue that cannot be ignored. Questions to ask include:

- Are bathrooms accessible for events in this location?

- If they aren't, where do people go?

- Are they located in hidden locations, where visitors will be vulnerable to attack?

- Does bathroom access mean the entire school must be left open during events, or can alternatives be arranged?

- Do the bathrooms show signs of abuse?

- Who locks and unlocks them?

- Is a key checkout arrangement conceivable for some types of events?

- Are double-door entries muffling sound to a point where teachers can't hear fights occurring? (Remedies include locking one door open, switching to a maze-entry design, or installing portable toilets.)

- Can bathrooms be built adjacent to the fields, accessible from outside without allowing access further into the school?

Classrooms

Classrooms were identified as the second most likely location for an in-school shooting in a 1990 study (*Caught in the Crossfire: A Report on Gun Violence in Our Nation's Schools* 1990), and they were the site of 9.5 percent of all school-associated violent deaths during the 1992-94 period (*Journal of the American Medical Association*, June 1996). This fact alone underscores the importance of CPTED applications in this arena. There are at least three critical areas to address in terms of classroom design:

1. **Access control.** Can the class be locked down at a moment's notice, or must the teacher first exit the room, insert a key in the knob, then re-enter the room? This is hardly an efficient action in a crisis. In fact, under high-stress circumstances, predictable physiological responses rob human beings of their fine-motor skills while preparing for "fight or flight." Fine-motor skills are precisely those needed to insert a key into a lock.

An emergency exit on the exterior wall of the classroom can be of great value. Does it automatically lock from the outside? An external door can also be a risk. In good weather, teachers often leave these doors ajar, providing easy access for offenders.

2. **Surveillance.** Can the teacher see what's going on in the classroom, the adjacent hallway, or nearby school grounds? Can staff members in the hallway easily see what's occurring in the classroom? Teachers frequently cover the small windows in their doors—if they exist at all—to restrict distractions.

3. **Territoriality.** Is the area directly outside the classroom marked in some way as semiprivate space? If not, intruders may feel comfortable loitering directly outside the classroom window. A developed patio, play space, or garden area helps establish this as outdoor classroom turf.

The bottom line is to think about what makes a room safe; these details are critical. A working PA system and/or a radio/cell phone can be just as essential as chalk and a blackboard.

Conclusion

The debate on just how far to go in securing schools is far from over. In the wake of highly publicized schoolyard massacres, some people will push for a high-security lockup architectural design. Others will insist that a well-designed school should look like a place to learn—not a locked-down fortress. Prudent application of CPTED principles can satisfy both perspectives.

Architectural features that allow school staff members to naturally see what's going on, to control access to the school, and to maintain control over the environment can make a tremendous difference, while enhancing, rather than detracting from, the learning environment.

Violence has now, unfortunately, become a common occurrence in our nation's schools; we deny or ignore this development at our peril. Schools can prevent much of this violence with good design, but they must also be prepared to immediately adjust security measures to match the level of risk anticipated or experienced on a daily basis. In most cases, schools are not now physically designed to deter violent behavior, nor are they prepared to take swift action in securing the school when dangerous situations arise. By applying CPTED concepts, they could be.

CHAPTER
5

Case Study Applications of CPTED Principles

This chapter illustrates how a school-safety assessment can be conducted with the use of Crime Prevention Through Environmental Design (CPTED) concepts and principles. Case studies by the senior author of two elementary schools demonstrate how to conduct CPTED assessments, how to evaluate and interpret the results, and how to apply the information to make the schools safer. The case studies describe actual schools whose names have been changed to maintain confidentiality.

St. Helena Elementary

St. Helena school, located within a medium-sized suburban school district (15,000 students), was built in 1904 along a narrow

The original entry is no longer used by visitors.

country byway surrounded by farmland. Almost a century later, the area now finds itself on the outskirts of a medium-sized city surrounded by small businesses and malls. A raised freeway that surrounds the city

passes a block away. A pub is located across the street.

The adjacent road has been expanded to a five-lane thoroughfare creating so much noise that school windows are kept closed. There is no space for a car or bus to stop at the front door anymore, so most school access is through the back lot. That also is where the district added new buildings—two portable classrooms along with several permanent structures—as the school site grew with the population.

Amid this scattered cluster of additional buildings is a long row of classrooms fronted by an open breezeway, in the style of a motel. Each classroom opens onto the breezeway, so there is no possibility of screening visitors to campus before they reach a chosen room. The one back driveway is clogged with traffic at student dropoff and pickup times.

The scattered buildings provide a warren of hidden areas that attract partying young adults, graffiti artists, skateboarders, and drug users on a nightly basis. There is no access control, the layout cuts off surveillance, and there are no indicators of territorial control.

Visitors, who primarily enter through the east (back) entrance, must walk through the entire school campus to even find the office, which is still located at the front of the building, waiting for the occasional visitor to arrive from the west. The office has no view of any classrooms, nor can it see 99 percent of the campus. A sign at the back entrance, wistfully holding on to a rapidly diminishing past, still denies access to horses.

CPTED Recommendations

1. Office Location. So that the office may regain its role as gatekeeper and have natural surveillance of the rest of the campus, it must be moved to the eastern side of the main school building. In such circumstances, the natural choice is to convert an existing space, such as a classroom or storage space, for office use, because the goals are to minimize construction costs and to preserve the look of the building.

Major road expansion has made it impossible for cars or buses to stop at the original main entry.

In this particular case, the new construction has already confused the look of the site to such a degree that preservation is no longer a reasonable concern. Any suitable existing space that faces east could be converted to office space.

If no such space can be found, a new office wing will need to be constructed, preferably in the center of the east (back) entrance. From this position, assuming that glass is used wherever possible, office staff can maintain extensive surveillance of the property and can effectively serve as gatekeeper. If all other doors automatically lock, visitors will be obliged to pass through the main office entry to gain access to the main hallway.

A portable building that is not well located needs to be moved out of the way to allow proper surveillance between the school buildings and the school entry area.

The office should also have access control over everyone who comes onto the property. That control can only be realized through the changes discussed below.

2. Scattered Buildings. The eastern side of the campus, with its handful of newer

The back lot is the main access point for most vehicle traffic.

fire exits could be alarmed as a deterrent. Solid walls would achieve maximum security and could be designed to match the brickwork of the original construction.

3. Motel-Style Classrooms. Moving the office and enclosing the courtyard still leave one problem unsolved: excessive access to the newer suite of classrooms whose doors open onto a breezeway. The solution is expensive but unavoidable if the school truly wants access control. The breezeway needs to be converted into a hallway, and the hallway needs to be connected to the main school building. Access to the hallway needs to be regulated by auto-locking doors (allowing use as emergency exits, or as needed by staff members who have keys), and signs should direct visitors to the new main entry for admittance.

buildings, is riddled with problems, highlighted by a water fountain that is encased in a padlocked wire-mesh cage. In addition, there are dead walls, blocked angles of surveillance, blind corners, multiple access points to the open areas adjacent to, into, and on top of the buildings. Mirrors and windows would do little good; the main problems occur after hours, when no authorized person is there to see anyway.

The easiest cure for this area would be to transform it into an enclosed, secured courtyard. Enclosing the courtyard eliminates all the problems at once. The site would no longer function as an afterhours hangout, nor could it be used as an access point onto the roof. Moreover, the courtyard could be used for outdoor activities more securely; sculpture or artwork is more likely to survive over time.

To create the enclosure, there are two options: tall wrought-iron fencing or solid walls, peppered with windows for surveillance. Fencing in this case would be a little awkward because of the need for fire exits. It's very difficult to secure fencing against intruders who can reach through and manipulate fire-exit hardware. Of course, the

Braddock Elementary

Braddock Elementary School, built in 1926, is similar in original design to St. Helena Elementary, but with different problems. Both schools started with a classic fortress design. Differences surfaced when St. Helena grew while Braddock remained basically the same size.

Braddock's weakest feature is the office, located in the middle of an east-west hallway. Its only natural-surveillance view is of the small slab of hallway directly adjacent to the office door entry. The location does not allow surveillance of the north-south

Critiques of Selected School Incidents: Could They Have Been Prevented Through Application of CPTED Principles?

■ **Jonesboro, Arkansas,** April 24, 1998—Two boys, ages 11 and 13, set off a fire alarm to draw Westside Middle School students outdoors. Dressed in camouflage outfits, the two boys hid in the woods nearby, then shot 15 people once the crowd had gathered outside, killing four. Two rifles and additional weapons were recovered. There was no apparent motive for the shootings. The boys were quite accurate in their fire as a result of having had extensive practice in simulated target shooting from playing video games. Many more injuries resulted as a consequence.

CPTED Analysis. The primary CPTED weakness in this scenario involves the nearby patch of woods, which apparently provided sufficient cover to camouflage the shooters. Any undeveloped turf near the school is an attractive location for illicit behavior. Perhaps if the woods had been clear of brush it would have helped. A fence between the school and the woods might have been somewhat beneficial, but only if it was untraversable. This might have restricted the boys in their ability to pull the alarm and then retreat into the forest.

Improvements in surveillance, by installing windows or mirrors, might have allowed staff to see the offenders pulling the alarm. Installing alarms only in viewable locations might have been worthwhile in discouraging their misuse. A protected evacuation site might have helped, as might the ability to quickly re-enter the school.

■ **West Paducah, Kentucky,** December 1, 1997—Mike Carneal, a 14-year-old student who had made intolerant remarks in the past, came to school armed with a pistol and shot 8 students who had gathered for a prayer group inside the main entrance. He was armed with a .22 caliber semiautomatic handgun with three spare clips of ammunition, two .22 caliber rifles, and two shotguns. Most of the weapons had been stolen in a burglary.

The long guns were hidden, wrapped and taped inside a quilt. He told a teacher, as well as his sister, who drove him to school, that the bundle was "an English project." He had previously told other students that "something big" would happen Monday. He

Continued on p. 75

hallway nearby. To compound the problem, the office is not located near any of the three main entrances, nor any of the informal entrances off the south playground area.

The south wall is primarily a solid, dead wall. It offers a number of entry points, including the back door to the kitchen/cafeteria area, the gym, a preschool, and at least one classroom. The building design at the southwest corner is a series of blind corners leading to the cafeteria entry and dumpster area. The south wall abuts a large field and playground area. A quiet residential zone bordering the university rings the entire site.

CPTED Recommendations

1. The Office Area. Three options, varying in expense, should be considered for the office area.

The first, least expensive option is to install convex mirrors to improve the office staff's surveillance up and down the east-west hallway, and to some extent around the corner and down the north-south hallway.

stood ten feet from his victims, inserted ear plugs, then fired methodically.

Seventeen-year-old Ben Strong disarmed him before he could fire the single bullet left in the clip. A teacher heading into the school from parking-lot duty "was six yards away from it—all of our students were running out and I was running in." Carneal said he had no particular vendetta. He is reported to have acted as if he had committed only a minor offense.

CPTED Analysis. There are insufficient data to suggest that anyone could have reasonably anticipated this attack. Only severe CPTED measures would have had a real impact here, with an armed guard, metal detectors, and/or a controlled-entry vestibule. However, in a school with no history of similar incidents, it would be unrealistic to expect a constant full-security alert. Without seeing the actual school layout, it is difficult to assess architectural weaknesses.

There is a slim chance that basic CPTED measures to reduce access—by holding the event deeper within the school, for example, while establishing restricted and monitored access—might have provided some degree of protection. Improved surveillance by staff would only have made a difference if the assailant's weapons were visible before he entered the school. In this case, with a teacher mere yards away, it's clear that adult staffing alone was not a significant factor.

Schoolwide measures aimed at establishing a positive school atmosphere might have helped, but there is no evidence that a negative climate was an issue. Any truly preventive remedies here would most likely have had to involve targeted intervention with Carneal himself.

■ **Edinboro, Pennsylvania**, April 26, 1998—Parker Middle School student Andrew Wurst, age 14, shot 4 people at an 8th-grade graduation dance. The incident began on a patio outside a banquet hall at "Nick's Place," an offcampus club. He then entered the building, fired more shots, left through a rear exit, and was arrested. His motive was unknown. One student described Wurst as looking "dead" and as a grim loner who never fully opened his eyes.

CPTED Analysis. In this case again, school CPTED measures would have been of no avail. If the club itself were to apply CPTED standards, they would have needed to control the turf outside their patio area by blocking access and heightening surveillance. The answer in this case seems to call for preventive behavior-management approaches and/or psychological treatment.

This limited solution falls into the category of "better than nothing."

The second option involves major construction: ballooning the office wall, the hallway, and the rooms across the hall, forming a banana shape. The hallway now bends around the office, and the office staff can directly see up and down the hallway, thanks to extensive use of glass. This option, probably the most expensive of the three, may be impractical if load-bearing walls are involved, and it still doesn't solve the access-control problem.

The third option also involves significant costs, but it is not as radical a redesign as the second option, and it does address the access-control problem. The office needs to change places with the classroom presently adjacent to the main entry, near the southwest corner of the building.

To allow surveillance, windows need to be installed looking into the entry vestibule from the new office, as well as looking out onto the east-west hallway and into one north-south hallway. Convex mirrors can still be used to supplement natural views, but the

Table 5-1

WEBSITES on School Safety, Violence Prevention, and CPTED

ERIC Clearinghouse on Educational Management
http://eric.uoregon.edu/trends_issues/safety/index.html

Institute on Violence and Destructive Behavior – University of Oregon
http://darkwing.uoregon.edu/~ivdb/index.html

International CPTED Association
http://www.cpted.net

International CPTED Association 1998 conferences papers
www.arch.vt.edu/crimeprev/pages/ConfPap.html

National Alliance for Safe Schools
www.safeschools.org/

National Association of Attorneys General/National School Boards Association KEEP SCHOOLS SAFE
www.keepschoolssafe.org

National Center for Education Statistics – Violence & Discipline Problems in U.S. Public Schools 1996-1997
http://nces.ed.gov/pubs98/violence

National Clearinghouse for Educational Facilities
www.edfacilities.org

National Education Association
www.nea.org

National Institute of Justice—publication on security technologies
www.ojp.usdoj.gov/nij/crimdocs.htm

National Institute on the Education of At-Risk Students
www.ed.gov/offices/OERI/At-Risk/

National Resource Center for Safe Schools
www.safetyzone.org

National School Safety Center
www.nssc1.org/

NEA Safe Schools Page
www.nea.org/issues/safescho/

Oregon School Boards Association – Crisis Management
www.OSBA.org/hotopics/crismgmt/index.htm

Ribbon of Promise
www.ribbonofpromise.org

Update Center for School Safety
www.MHRCC.org/scss/links.html

U.S. Office of Juvenile Justice and Delinquency Prevention
www.ojjdp.ncjrs.org

U.S. Office of Safe and Drug Free Schools
www.ed.gov/offices/OESE/SDFS

Web of Justice
www.co.pinellas.fl.us/bcc/juscoord/ejuvenile.htm

office now has extensive natural surveillance inside at least two hallways, inside the entry vestibule, and directly outside through the existing windows in the north wall.

The window into the entry vestibule should slide open to allow staff to communicate with visitors. If additional security were desired, the vestibule could be enclosed by installing a second set of entry doors with electronic locks; to gain entry to the hallways, visitors would enter after being buzzed-in by office staff. If conditions warrant, the outer entry doors could incorporate metal detectors.

All other entry points into the school need to automatically lock, and clearly written, bilingual signs should direct visitors to the main office entry.

2. The South Wall. The south wall of the school is largely comprised of dead walls, though there are some exceptions. It has at least two very weak areas in terms of access control—a covered bike-storage area that's nestled into the center of the south wall and that adjoins an entry door, and the kitchen area, with its series of blind corners and easy school access.

One solution improves surveillance to the south while also enlarging the kitchen, which is so small that two people cannot pass each other without brushing up against the stove. The design would extend the kitchen wall outward, tracing an arc that encompasses the series of blind corners. The kitchen should have windows looking out into the south field, thereby improving natural surveillance.

The bike-storage area is a dark and foreboding place, imbedded beneath the building, roughly below the library, and accessed from the south. There is no natural surveillance into this area, which is effectively sealed off both visually and physically. Access should be improved by replacing the damaged mesh fence with wrought iron and installing motion-detector lights to highlight afterhours intruders. The hidden entry should be locked when not staffed. Ideally, the bike racks should be moved to the front of the building, directly outside the new main office windows, and adjacent to the main entry.

6

The Role of Architects
in School Design

*A*rchitects *bring exceptional expertise to the task of designing and retrofitting schools to make them safer. For example, architects can assess whether various options will satisfy building codes, and they can translate key concepts and needs into blueprints.*

Unfortunately, architects do not routinely seek out training in CPTED, and CPTED analysts are not consistently invited to instruct architects and planners as part of their academic programs. It is not unusual for architects to reject input from CPTED analysts on the grounds that architects "have been building schools for decades." Most of the schools constructed over the past century are woefully inadequate from a CPTED perspective, built in an era when school shootings and rampant, on-campus drug dealing were unheard-of occurrences.

CPTED analysts routinely review plans, or inspect new buildings, and find flaws that could easily have been fixed if caught in time. To cite two such errors noted by the senior author recently:

1. One state-of-the-art juvenile detention facility positioned the guard at the metal detector, but installed the elevator to the courtrooms directly behind him. This meant all visitors were empowered to walk a few feet behind him, out of his field of vision—creating a very uncomfortable and potentially hazardous situation for security personnel.

2. Another new, multimillion-dollar, high-tech detention facility installed a two-story front wall of glass facing south. This resulted in overexposure to the sun on bright

days, blinding any staff looking in that direction, completely undermining their natural surveillance of the entry walkway and parking lot. Staff had temporarily addressed this problem by taping black plastic garbage bags over some of the window panes.

Many schools today were built decades ago with an anticipated lifespan of no more than fifty years and are now falling apart; many suffer from deferred maintenance due to budget shortfalls. Design flaws, use of building materials now known to create hazards, and inadequate maintenance have all led to unanticipated costs. Flat roofs require hot-mopping on a regular basis, lead paint and asbestos pose health hazards, and moldy carpets contribute to a high rate of asthma among students.

In the year 2000 an International Building Code (IBC) will be introduced, with an expectation that it will be adopted gradually yet broadly. That process may take a few years; in the meantime many states, including Oregon, will continue to operate under current regulations. Even when the IBC is widely adopted, state and local legislation may require certain amendments to the code.

Improvements that might seem simple, such as connecting buildings with wrought-iron fencing, encounter building-code requirements of some complexity. The newly connected buildings may be considered as one large building under the code, and that designation triggers certain standards in terms of fire and other life-safety concerns.

The more flammable the construction material, the smaller a building is allowed to be. In many cases, schools are built of less expensive, more highly combustible materials to stretch budgets. However, some factors can be manipulated to allow for a larger overall building. These variables include, for example, the amount of empty space around the building; the construction materials used (brick, steel, and concrete buildings, in many respects, have no size limits, whereas 2 x 4 construction may be limited to as few as 9,600 square feet); the installation of sprinklers; or the construction of firewalls to protect one section of the new building from fire in another section.

In many cases, it is more cost-effective to build an entirely new facility than it is to retrofit an old one, especially when viewed over a planned lifespan of 50 to 75 years. Although new materials may bring hazards as well—such as new carpets and glues that require "off-gassing" for days or weeks— there are now environmentally friendly materials that provide healthy alternatives.*

Exploding enrollment, availability of new technology, excessive maintenance costs, health hazards, corroded pipes, energy-inefficient design, low-end construction materials, and CPTED weaknesses can provide compelling justification to support bond measures for new school construction.

*One source of information about these new materials is Environmental Building Supplies at www. EcoHaus.com (503-222-3881).

Any competent architect will be sensitive to these issues and receptive to new information. Health, safety, and CPTED concepts can easily be incorporated into school designs. In addition, they can be used to assess the cost-efficiency of architectural alternatives, helping to determine at what point new construction becomes more economical than remodeling or retrofitting.

Examples of the work of architects who are applying CPTED concepts are illustrated on the following pages. In the first set of drawings (figures 6-1 and 6-2), Eugene, Oregon, architect Ed Waterbury has taken the CPTED recommendations for St. Helena Elementary (see previous chapter) and incorporated them into a number of design alternatives that address key security concerns while trying to contain costs as much as possible.

Another example is a 3D perspective created by Springfield, Oregon, architect Arturo Paz of A. Paz Architects. His three-dimensional computer models illustrate an approach to design that allows a walk-through of the school site and its buildings. This modeling improves the capacity for noting CPTED flaws and correcting them almost immediately, such as by adding a window, curving a wall, or removing a visual obstacle. This approach has enormous potential for detecting errors early in the design stage, rather than waiting until after the building has been constructed (see illustrations).

In Mr. Paz's work it becomes apparent to the viewer that:

- Visitors will be visible to office staff as soon as they enter the parking lot.
- Visitors will be obligated to use the main entrance to gain entry to the school.
- Office staff members have an opportunity to scrutinize visitors and electronically lock doors if this is warranted.

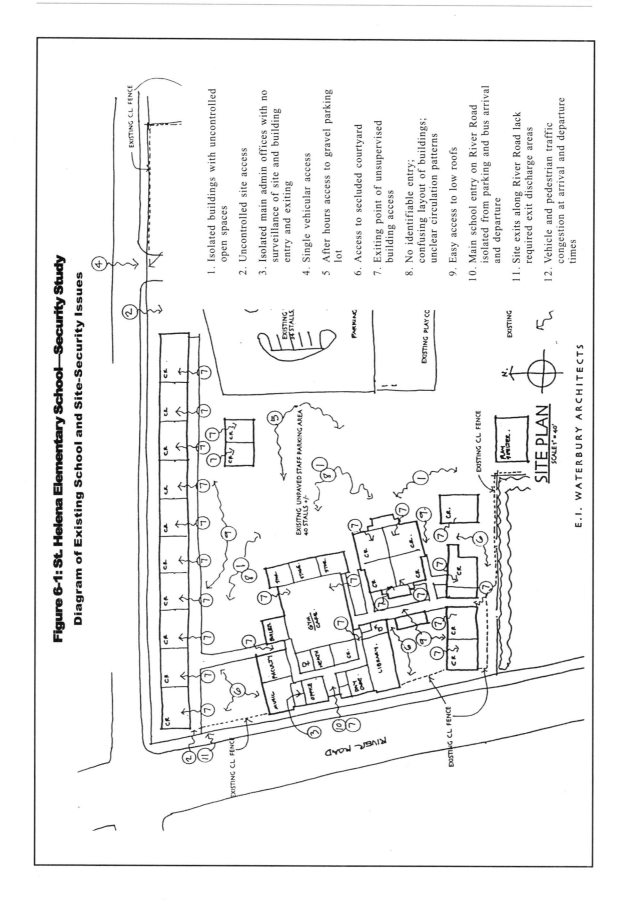

Figure 6-1: St. Helena Elementary School—Security Study
Diagram of Existing School and Site-Security Issues

1. Isolated buildings with uncontrolled open spaces

2. Uncontrolled site access

3. Isolated main admin offices with no surveillance of site and building entry and exiting

4. Single vehicular access

5. After hours access to gravel parking lot

6. Access to secluded courtyard

7. Exiting point of unsupervised building access

8. No identifiable entry; confusing layout of buildings; unclear circulation patterns

9. Easy access to low roofs

10. Main school entry on River Road isolated from parking and bus arrival and departure

11. Site exits along River Road lack required exit discharge areas

12. Vehicle and pedestrian traffic congestion at arrival and departure times

SITE PLAN
SCALE 1" = 40'

E.I. WATERBURY ARCHITECTS

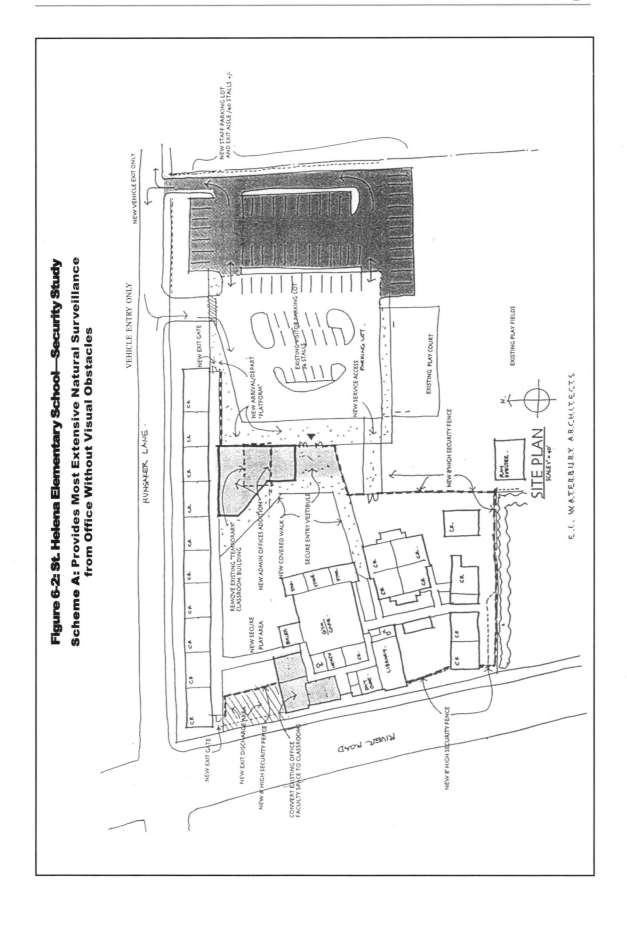

Figure 6-2: St. Helena Elementary School—Security Study
Scheme A: Provides Most Extensive Natural Surveillance
from Office Without Visual Obstacles

Table 6-1

Scheme A: St. Helena Elementary

Description

Reorganize school's administrative offices and faculty spaces for more direct visual supervision of students and visitors by:

- Removing existing "temporary" classroom building
- Constructing new building for administrative offices and faculty spaces
- Converting existing administrative offices and faculty spaces to classrooms
- Constructing new secure entry vestibule
- Constructing new covered walkways

Create a secure and defined "campus" environment with formalized and central entrance.

Provide 8' HGT security fencing (open and fitting into character of the school).

Create a recognizable arrival and departure "platform" (safe and weather protected place for loading and unloading bus).

Relocate unpaved staff parking area to new paved parking expansion to existing visitor parking lot.

Provide a new site vehicle exit aisle and exit to Hunsaker Lane; Convert existing site vehicle entry/exit to entry only.

Estimated Costs

1. Remove existing "temporary" classroom building		$10,000	+/-
2. Construct new administrative offices and faculty spaces building	(2700 s.f. +/-)	$270,000	+/-
3. Convert existing administrative offices and faculty space to classrooms	(1500 s.f. +/-)	$375,000	+/-
4. Construct new secure entry vestibule	(1000 s.f. +/-)	$25,000	+/-
5. Construct new covered walkways	(170 l.f. +/-)	$32,300	+/-
6. Site improvements			
• New arrival/depart "platform"	(2900 s.f. +/-)	$14,500	+/-
• Renovate existing staff gravel parking lot area		$2,500	+/-
• New 8' HGT perimeter fencing ornamental iron or chain link	(500 l.f. +/-) (Range)	$5,000 $27,000	+/- +/-
• New paved staff parking lot expansion and exit aisle	(16,500 s.f.+/-)	$52,700	+/-
• General landscape improvements		$2500	+/-

Total estimated rough construction costs   **$816,500**

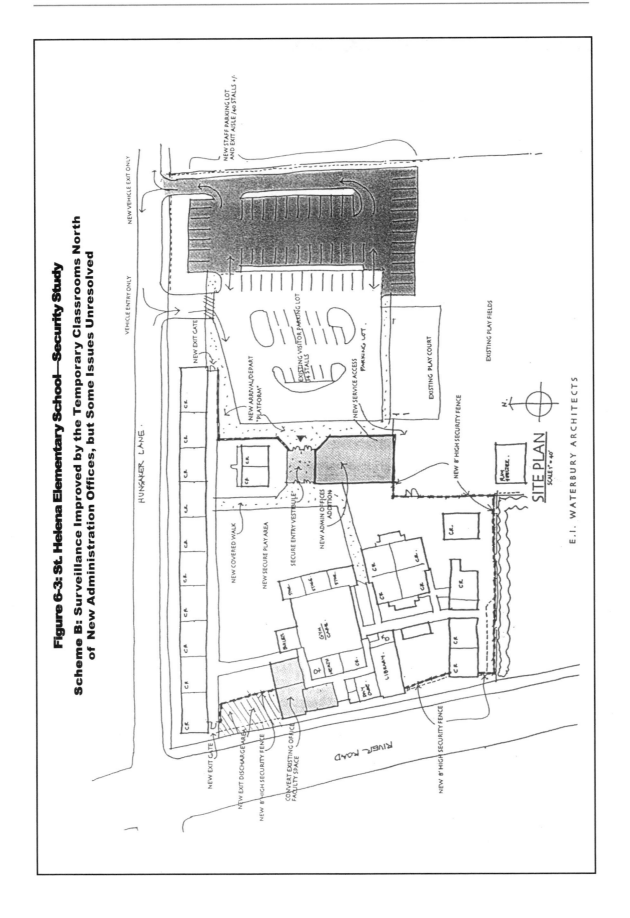

Figure 6-3: St. Helena Elementary School—Security Study

Scheme B: Surveillance Improved by the Temporary Classrooms North of New Administration Offices, but Some Issues Unresolved

Table 6-2

Scheme B: St. Helena Elementary

Description

Reorganize school's administrative offices and faculty spaces for more direct visual supervision of students and visitors by:

- Construct new building for administrative offices and faculty spaces.
- Construct new secure entry vestibule.
- Convert existing administrative office and faculty spaces to classrooms.
- Construct new covered walkways.

Create a secure and defined "campus" environment with formalized and central entrance.

Provide 8' HGT security fencing (open and fitting into character of the school).

Create a recognizable arrival and departure "platform" (safe and weather protected place for loading and unloading bus).

Relocate unpaved staff parking area to new paved parking expansion to existing visitor parking lot.

Provide a new site vehicle exit aisle and exit to Hunsaker Lane; convert existing site vehicle entry/exit to entry only.

Estimated Costs

1. Construct new administrative offices and faculty space building	(2500 s.f.+/-)	$250,000 +/-
2. Construct new secure entry vestibule	(600 s.f. +/-)	$15,000 +/-
3. Convert existing administrative offices and faculty space	(1500 s.f. +/-)	$37,500 +/-
4. New covered walkways	(185 l.f. +/-)	$35,000 +/-
5. General site improvements		
• New arrival/depart "platform"	(2900 s.f. +/-)	$14,500 +/-
• Renovate existing staff gravel parking lot area		$2,500 +/-
• New 8' HGT perimeter fencing ornamental iron or chain link	(521 l.f. +/-) (range)	$5,200 +/- $26,000 +/-
• New paved staff parking lot expansion and exit aisle	(16500 s.f. +/-)	$52,700 +/-
• General landscape improvements		$2500 +/-

Total estimated rough construction costs $440,900

• Office staff members have excellent natural surveillance, both within the facilities and outside the fenced area.

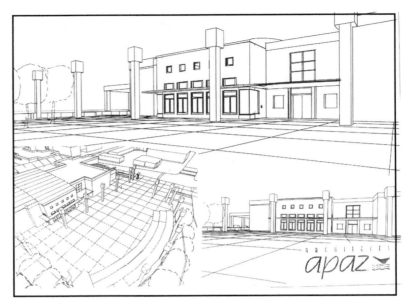

Three-dimensional computer models by A. Paz Architects allow designers to note and correct CPTED flaws.

CHAPTER

7

Policy Recommendations
for School Districts

Familiarity with Crime Prevention Through Environmental Design (CPTED) concepts puts school boards and administrators in a stronger position to mitigate risks and improve safety and security at school. Familiarity without follow-through, however, is an awkward equation when it comes to liability. If problems are foreseeable, it is wise not to ignore them but rather to take prudent action to prevent them.

Unfortunately, most schools were built without awareness of CPTED concepts, and the cost of remodeling these schools to the highest standards is far beyond the budgetary capacities of the vast majority of districts throughout the country.

A recent National Center for Education Statistics report estimated it will cost the nation about $127 billion for long-delayed repairs and additions to school facilities (Richard 2000). To bring the nation's schools into compliance with CPTED concepts, making them safer places in which to work and learn, would push this figure even higher.

The question then becomes how to even begin to address an overwhelming price tag for infrastructure upkeep with equally urgent staffing and supply expenses and at the same time tackle school-security concerns. For school boards wishing to embrace CPTED concepts, an appropriate policy must respond to needs in two broad categories: (1) future construction and (2) maintenance of existing structures.

Future Construction

Depending on local priorities, a school district can adopt guidelines that range from the extremely broad to the site-specific. Some examples of possible policies are as follows:

1. The school board or central office may want to adopt a resolution that all future construction in the district shall meet with basic CPTED standards for school security.

2. The school board may want to go a step further and specify that a trained CPTED inspector will review and approve all construction projects. This inspector can be a district employee with specialized training or an independent contractor with CPTED expertise. In either case the expertise must be documented to the satisfaction of the superintendent of schools or another designated authority. Qualified inspectors and trainers can be reached through the International CPTED Association (www.cpted.net).

3. The school board may desire to specify particular design features that must be in-

Security Ideas for New School Design

The National Institute of Justice recently published a very helpful guide for schools and law-enforcement agencies titled *The Appropriate and Effective Use of Security Technologies in U.S. Schools: A Guide for Practical School Security Applications*, by Mary W. Green (1999). This guide is highly recommended. The full text of the guide is available electronically (in ASCII text, Adobe Acrobat, and HTML) at http://www.ojp.usdoj.gov/nij/crimdocs.htm

The following excerpt from the guide suggests ideas to keep in mind when designing a new school facility.

Although this list includes only a few basic security technologies (such as cameras, sensors, and so forth), the facility design should not preclude their straightforward installation in the future.

- Limit the number of buildings—one building is best—to limit outsiders on the campus.

- Minimize the entrances to the school building—having one or two main entrances/exits will support efforts to keep outsiders off campus. Allow enough room at the main entry in the event that a screening area (i.e., for weapon or drug detection) needs to be incorporated later on. Alarm other exits for emergency use only.

- Minimize the line of sight from secluded off-campus sites onto student gathering areas, the main entry doors, playgrounds, patios, and so forth . . . . (This suggestion must be tempered against the benefits gained from the natural, desirable surveillance by neighbors, passers-by, officers on patrol, and so forth).

- Allow for a security person to be posted at a single entrance onto campus to chal-

lenge each vehicle for identification of all occupants. Buses and school employees should have a separate (and controlled) entrance.

- Provide a dropoff/pickup lane for buses only.

- Minimize the number of driveways or parking lots that students will have to walk across to get to the school building.

- Build single-stall bathrooms to mitigate bathroom confrontations and problems.

- Enclose the campus. (This is more a measure to keep outsiders out rather than to keep insiders in.) Beside defining property boundaries, a robust fence forces a perpetrator to consciously trespass, rather than allowing casual entry.

- Make certain that the school building and classroom areas can be closed and locked off from the gym and other facilities used during off hours.

- Minimize secluded hiding places for un-

Continued on p. 89

cluded in all new construction in the district. Some reasonable specifications include the following:

- A front office shall be located adjacent to the front doors, with a level of security equal to or greater than level 5 on the Schneider scale (see page 61)

- All entrances will be designed to allow access control and surveillance capability.

- Bathrooms will be designed to allow for a maze-entry option wherever possible.

If, instead of specifying particulars, the board wants to couch its CPTED policy in general terms, it can state a few broad guidelines, such as a requirement that all designs demonstrate reasonable integration of natural surveillance and natural access-control considerations.

authorized persons, both inside and outside buildings.

- Do not eliminate windows, but use them strategically. Consider incorporating clerestories or secure skylights that allow light in but that are less vulnerable than typical windows.

- Maximize the line of sight within buildings.

- Large wide spaces, like hallways or commons, should have sufficient vertical dimension so space does not feel restrictive to students.

- Consider installing student lockers in classrooms or other areas easy to monitor so that there is no single locker area that becomes a bottleneck, and there is always the deterrence of an adult nearby . . . .

- Do not cut corners on communications, especially those required for security. Make certain that your facility has built in the necessary receivers and transmitters throughout the structure to allow for dependable two-way radio and cellular phone use. (Sometimes radio frequency communication is not possible deep within a large, structurally dense facility.)

- Where possible, have buildings and other student gathering areas set back from the streets, driveways, or parking areas by at least 50 feet.

- Install a basic security alarm system throughout all hallways, administrative

offices, and rooms containing high-value property, such as computers, VCRs, shop equipment, laboratory supplies, and musical instruments.

- Allow a law enforcement officer to live on campus. (In some school districts, an officer is allowed to move his or her own trailer to a strategic location on campus and receive free utilities in exchange for prenegotiated and formally contracted responsibilities.) The deterrent effect of a police vehicle parked on campus all night and weekend can be great. Such an arrangement can also provide both detection and response in situations where damage is being inflicted upon the facility, but no alarm system would normally detect it . . . .

- Provide a separate parking area for work-study students or those who will be leaving during the school day. (This allows the main student parking lot to be closed off during the school day.)

- Make certain that exterior lighting is sufficient for safety. Lights mounted on the exterior of buildings often are inadequate for adjoining driveways or parking lots.

- Do not underestimate the value of trees and landscaping on a school campus. An attractive, well maintained school is generally less attractive to thieves.

SOURCE: Green (1999). *The Appropriate and Effective Use of Security Technologies in U.S. Schools, A Guide for Practical School Security Applications.* Washington D.C.: National Institute of Justice, U.S. Department of Justice, September 1999. 129 pages.

Maintenance of Existing Structures

This part of the policy task is more difficult for most school boards, because it requires prioritizing CPTED improvements for existing schools. The choices boil down to pocketbook issues: it's a rare school district that can implement all the necessary or recommended CPTED alterations in all

their schools. One approach would be as follows:

1. Arrange to have all schools inspected. These inspections should be conducted with consistency, ideally by the same inspector using the same standards throughout. Communicate with CPTED analysts well ahead of time to determine likely costs, which can then be incorporated into grant

Installing office windows might be a priority districtwide.

5. Decide whether, as a prerequisite for receiving CPTED dollars, schools must take steps to improve their social ecology. Schools may be required, for example, to establish an effective behavior-support plan, institute a violence-prevention curriculum, or demonstrate a commitment to school improvement that might be worth supporting with physical measures.

When school districts have limited dollars to spend and have decided to fix only a few schools rather than spread the funds so thin that they would have little impact, here are some considerations that may be useful in identifying candidates for limited CPTED funding:

- Other maintenance, repair, and longevity considerations make spending money on this particular building a worthwhile investment. In other words, this project would not involve throwing money down a black hole.

- This school has a history of significant behavioral problems, with students, staff, families, or visitors, which heightens the need for security measures.

- School has a history of significant property crimes that would justify investing in security measures.

- The school population exhibits significant risk factors—low socioeconomic status, high mobility, high percentage of special-education students—that are frequently associated with problem behaviors.

requests. The inspector should produce a report itemizing recommended improvements throughout the district, regardless of cost.

2. Arrange for rough estimates of costs for the recommended improvements.

3. Establish a fiscal plan to address these recommendations consistent with the budgetary realities of your school district. This might involve pursuing state, federal, or private funds, or it might involve parceling out improvements over a period of ten to twenty years.

4. Where funds are limited, schools should determine:

- which improvements are critical in the short run (for example, upgrade all faulty public-address systems)

- which improvements should be applied districtwide (for example, install convex mirrors wherever effective to eliminate blind spots; install windows in offices where it would make a significant difference in surveillance; convert all breezeways into enclosed hallways, restricting outside access)

- which schools should be fixed first (for example, it may make more sense to fix one school well than all schools poorly)

Figure 7-1

Elements of School Security

This diagram depicts things to consider when designing a new security system for a school environment that can be used against various threats. Some examples of each component are included.

Consequences

- Suspension/ expulsion

- Mandatory work on campus

- Citation or arrest by law enforcement officer

- Judicial system

Response/ Investigation

- Security personnel

- Law enforcement

- Viewing videotapes

- Reward offered for information

Delay

- Bolted-down equipment

- Locked doors

- Fences

Detection

- Sensors

- Drug dogs

- Bomb dogs

- Cameras

- Duress alarms

- Weapon screenings

- Student "hotlines" or crimestopper programs

- Drug swipes

- Staff in strategic locations

Deterrence

- Fencing

- Signs

- Reputation

- Video cameras

- I.D. checks

- Weapon screenings

- Officer(s) on campus

- Thorny bushes

- Antigraffiti sealers

- Random locker searches

- Vehicle checks

- Drug dogs

SOURCE: Green (1999). *The Appropriate and Effective Use of Security Technologies in U.S. Schools, A Guide for Practical School Security Applications*. Washington D.C.: National Institute of Justice, U.S. Department of Justice, September 1999. 129 pages. www.ojp.usdoj.gov/nij/crimdocs.htm.

• The surrounding neighborhood has a high crime rate, which correlates with greater risks for students approaching or leaving the school.

Security Technology

The school board may or may not want to separate funding for technology from funding for structural changes. Districts are often better off buying a small amount of higher quality security technology, and sharing this between schools, than looking for bargains that are less effective. Be mindful that today's technology will be obsolete in a year or two; don't lock in to specific technology to be purchased five years from now.

Pay careful attention to maintenance needs for technical equipment; ideally send at least two maintenance staff for training in equipment maintenance and repair. Make sure that your purchase source includes a local maintenance arrangement.

The following list of technology options is for illustrative purposes and may not necessarily include the best choices for a particular district.

1. Install electronic controls, doorbells, and/or intercoms on front doors where they can be integrated into an appropriate access-control layout.
2. Buy one set of wireless high-sensitivity flame detectors to be moved between schools as the need arises, to address problems with smoking in the bathrooms.

3. Invest in districtwide message-paging systems to alert staff members during crises.
4. Buy cell phones and/or radios for all campus supervisors.
5. Buy portable metal-detection equipment to be moved into schools as needed.
6. Buy one portable security-camera system, to be moved to troublesome locations as the need arises.

Common Errors

1. *Wholesale prescriptions.* Each school faces unique challenges, with distinctive architecture, budgets, maintenance needs, staff, parents, student bodies, political climates, and levels of support. Suggesting that

Poor preplanning resulted in fencing being added to prevent falls into the stairwell; razor wire was added to block access to the roof.

one model would solve every school's security problems is akin to treating every medical condition with the same drug. Smalltown, U.S.A., is not the same as East L.A. School boards, knowing the particular challenges facing their own communities and schools, are in the best position to prescribe solutions to fit unique local needs.

2. *Hasty, mismatched problems and solutions.* People are quick to propose solutions immediately after an incident has oc-

curred, when parents are angry and administrators want to demonstrate that they are taking action. Some of the most common errors in this regard involve installation of fencing and metal detectors. Before making major investments in these "solutions," it is productive to carefully identify the problems the district most commonly faces and decide exactly what should be done about them.

Fencing, for example, can be a great tool for limiting access, but it's not always the best solution to the problem of unauthorized access. If students are now forced to walk all the way around the fence to get to school, are they perhaps even more likely to be victimized? Are they isolated during this walk? Are intruders cutting across the school grounds actually the problem you are facing? In many cases the problem visitors are coming through the main entrance.

If metal detectors are installed, who is going to staff them? Must other staff positions be cut to fund these new positions? Can students just as easily enter through another door, making the metal detector a waste of time and money? What are the metal detectors supposed to deter?

Answers to these kinds of questions should be sought prior to any decision to commit a school district or a school to these or any other security options.

Conclusion

The physical aspects of CPTED discussed in this book, complemented by curricula, attitudes and beliefs, and behaviors that create a social ecology of nonviolence and mutual respect, can transform a school from a war zone to a safe haven for all involved. These elements can make our schools safer, more functional, and more economical to operate. If staff members can efficiently control access to the school, maintain natural surveillance over the site, and nurture a sense of identity within the school community, the school will be a safer and more effective setting for educators and students.

Recommended Resources
for Enhancing School Safety
and Security

*L*isted below are some recommended resources for improving the safety and security of schools. They address procedures that involve architectural changes, the optional use and supervision of school space, technological innovations to improve security, and behavioral-instructional interventions for creating a more effective school with a positive climate.

A Gentle Deterrent to Vandalism by James Wise, *Psychology Today,* September, 1982.

Antisocial Behavior in School: Strategies and Best Practices, by Hill Walker, Geoff Colvin, and Elizabeth Ramnsey. Pacific Grove, California: Brooks/Cole, 1995. 481 pages.

Reduction of School Violence: Alternatives to Suspension. (2nd Edition) by Beverley Johns, Valerie Carr, and Charles Hoots, LRP Publications, Horsham, PA, 1995.

Applying Positive Behavioral Support and Functional Behavioral Assessment in Schools, Technical Assistance Guide # 1, available from the OSEP Center on Positive Behavioral Interventions and Supports, go to http://pbis.org., 1999

B. E. S. T. Building Effective Schools Together: A Three Tiered Approach to Safe, Effective, and Healthy School.. Eugene, Oregon: Institute on Violence and Destructive Behavior. Contact Rebecca Scarola, 1265 University of Oregon, Eugene, OR 97403-1265

Caught in the Crossfire: A Report on Gun Violence in Our Nation's Schools, Center to Prevent Handgun Violence, 1990.

Classroom Environment, by Barry J. Frase. London; Dover, New Hampshire:Croom Helm, 1986. 226 pages.

Confronting Violence on Buses, by James D. King, American School & University, June 1997 v69.

Creating an Inviting Classroom Environment, by Elizabeth S. Foster-Harrison and Ann Adams-Bullock. Bloomington; Indiana: Phi Delta Kappa Educational Foundation, 1998. 38 pages.

Creating Safe and Drug-Free Schools: An Action Guide. Washington, D.C. U.S. Department of Education, Division of Safe an1d Drug-Free Schools, 400 Md. Ave., S.W., Washington, D.C. 20202-6123.

Creating Safe Schools; What Principals Can Do, by Marie Somers Hill and Frank W. Hill. Thousand Oaks California, Corwin Press, 1994. 132 pages.

Crime Prevention Through Environmental Design, by Timothy D. Crowe. Boston: Butterworth-Heinemann, 1991. 241 pages.

Crisis Prevention and Response: Is Your School Prepared? by Cathy Paine and Jeffrey Sprague, Institute on Violence and Destructive Behavior, Oregon School Study Council Bulletin, available from the Oregon School Study Council, 213 Education Bldg., 1571 Alder St., College of Education, 1215 University of Oregon, Eugene, OR 97403-1215

Defensible Space: Deterring Crime and Building Community, by Henry G. Cisneros.Rockville, Maryland: U.S. Department of Housing and Urban Development, 1995. (free copies available from HUD at 1-800-245-2691).

Designing Places for Learning, edited by Anne Meek. Alexandria; Virginia: Association for Supervision and Curriculum Development, and Scottsdale, Arizona: The Council of Educational Facility Planners, International, 1995. 101 pages.

The Development of Competence in Favorable and Unfavorable Environments; Lessons from Research on Successful Children, by Ann S. Masten and J. Douglas Coatsworth, American Psychologist, 1998.

Drawing in the Family; Family Involvement in the Schools, Education Commission of the States, 1988.

Early Warning/Timely Response; A Guide to Safe Schools, Center for Effective collaboration and Practice of the American Institutes for Research in collaboration with the National Association of School Psychologists, 1998. http://www.ed.gov/offices/OSERS/OSEP/earlywrn.html

Environmental Design & Premises Liability Series: NIJ Research in Brief, by Corey L.Gordon, partner in the Mass Tort department of Robins, Kaplan, Miller & Ciresi. April 1996. (http:www.ncjrs.org/txtfiles/cptedlia.txt)

First Step to Success: Helping Young Children Overcome Antisocial Behavior, by Hill M. Walker, Kate Kavanagh, Annemieke Golly, Bruce Stiller, Herb Severson, and Edward Feil. Longmont, CO: Sopris West, Inc., 1997.

Florida School CPTED Guidelines. Available on the internet at: www.arch.usf.edu/flctr/projects/safesc/intro.htm.

High Schools or High-Tech Prisons?By Del Stover, *Education Digest,* Set 1994 v60.

Interior Design with Feng Shui, by Sarah Rossbach, Penguin Arkana, 1987

Lessons in Survival, by Karen N. Peart, Scholastic Update, Feb. 11, 1994 v126.

Making Schools Safer and Violence Free, by Hill M. Walker and Michael H. Epstein, Austin, TX: PRO-ED, Inc. September, 2000.

National Association of Elementary School Principals National Poll, 1997

NIJ Research in Brief; Crime Prevention Through Environmental Design in Parking Facilities, by Mary Smith (http://www.ncjrs.org/txtfiles/cptedpkg.txt).

The Other Side of School Violence: Educator Policies and Practices That May Contribute to Student Misbehavior, by Irwin A. Hyman and Donna C. Perone. *Journal of School Psychology,* Vol. 36, No.1, pp. 7-27, 1998.

The Power of Place; How Our Surroundings Shape Our Thoughts, Emotions and Actions, by Winifred Gallagher. Poseidon Press, 1993.

Preventing Crime: What Works, What Doesn't, What's Promising, Research in Brief. National Institute of Justice. by Lawrence W. Sherman, Denise Gottfredson, et al. 1998 (www.ncjrs.org/works/). 21 pages. ED 423 321.

Reinvesting in America, by Robin Garr. Reading, Massachusetts. Addison-Wesley, 1995. 271 pages.

Resolving Conflict Creatively: Evaluating the Developmental Effects of a School-Based Violence Prevention Program in Neighborhood and Classroom Context, by J. Lawrence Aber, Stephanie M. Jones, Joshua L. Brown, Nina Chaudry, and Faith Samples, *Development and Psychopathology, 10,* Cambridge University Press, 1998.

Safe by Design: Planning for Peaceful School Communities, by Sarah Miller, Janine Brodine, and Terri Miller. Available from the Committee for Children, Seattle, Washington, 2203 Airport Way South, Suite 500, Seattle, Washington 98134-2027, September, 1996.

Safe, Drug-Free, and Effective Schools for ALL Students by Mary Quinn, David Osher, and Catherine Hoffman, American Institutes for Research, Center for Effective Collaboratiion and Practice, OERI, 1000 Thomas Jefferson St., N. W., Suite 400, Washington, D.C. 20007. 1998.

School and Community Interventions to Prevent Serious and Violent Offending, U.S. Department of Justice, OJJDP, by Shay Bilchik, Administrator, 810 7th St., N.W., Washington, D.C., 20531.

School and Community Partnerships: Reforming Schools, Revitalizing Communities, by Michelle Cahill, Cross City Campaign for Urban School Reform, 407 South Dearborn Street, Suite 1725, Chicago, Il. 60605.(312) 322 3880.

School Safety: Promising Initiatives for Addressing School Violence. Report to the Ranking Minority Member, Subcommittee on Children and Families, Committee on Labor and Human Resources US Senate. 48 pages. ED 384 125. http://www.calyx.net/~schaffer/GOVPUBS/gao/gao15.html

Second Step: A Violence Prevention Curriculum. Seattle, Washington: Committee for Children, 2203 Airport Way South, Suite 500, Seattle, Washington 98134-2027. 1992. 109 pages. ED 350 542.

Security Efforts Cut Chicago-School Violence, by Debra Williams, Education Digest, Nov. 1995, v61 n3 p.18.

Setting Up a Class for the Most Disruptive Students, by Peter Martin Commanday, *Education Digest* 59. (Jan 1994).

Systemic Violence in Education; Promise Broken, edited by Juanita Ross Epp and Ailsa M. Watkinson, Albany, New York: State University of New York Press, 1997. 220 pages.

Teachers' Presence May Deter Violence, *USA Today* 125, 2619 (Dec. 1996). 13.

Teaching Teachers to Protect Themselves and Their Students, by Julie L. Nicklin, *Chronicle of Higher Education*, 42,33 (April 26, 1996).

The Acting Out Child: Coping with Classroom Disruption. by Hill M. Walker. (Second edition),Longmont, Colorado: Sopris West, Inc., 1995. 465 pages.

The Appropriate and Effective Use of Security Technologies in U.S. Schools: A Guide for Schools and Law Enforcement Agencies, by Mary Green. Washington, DC: US Dept. of Justice, Office of Justice Programs, National Institute of Justice.September, 1999. (Available through U.S. Dept. of Justice, OJJDP, 810 7th St. N.W., Washington, D.C. 20531. 129 pages.

The Science of Building Peace: How School Climate Can Prevent or Increase Substance Abuse and Violent Crime, by Dennis Embry, Ph.D., Heartsprings, Inc. 1997. (Ph 1-800-368-9356; e-mail: custrel@Heartsprings.org)

Violence Prevention and School Safety: Issues, Problems, Approaches, and Recommended Solutions, by Hill M. Walker, Larry K. Irvin and Jeffrey R. Sprague, Oregon School Study Council, University of Oregon,1997.

What Works in Reducing Adolescent Violence: An Empirical Review of the Field, by Patrick Tolan and Nancy Guerra, Center for the Study and Prevention of Violence, Institute for Behavioral Sciences, University of Colorado, Boulder, CO, 80309-0442.

White House Annual Report on School Safety (produced annually), available from the U.S. Office of Safe and Drug-Free Schools, U.S. Department of Education, 400 Md. Ave., S.W., Washington, D.C. 20202-6123.

Youth Violence Prevention, by Kenneth Powell and Darnell Hawkins, American Journal of Preventive Medicine, Supplement to Vol. 12, Number 5, September/October 1996.

Appendices

A. **National School Safety Center's School Crime Assessment Tool**

B. **Oregon School Safety Survey**

National School Safety Center's School Crime Assessment Tool

The National School Safety Center has developed the following school-crime assessment tool to assist school administrators in evaluating their vulnerability to school-crime issues and potential school-climate problems.

1. Has your community crime rate increased over the past 12 months?
2. Are more than 15% of your work-order repairs vandalism-related?
3. Do you have an open campus?
4. Has there been an emergence of an underground student newspaper?
5. Is your community transiency rate increasing?
6. Do you have an increasing presence of graffiti in your community?
7. Do you have an increased presence of gangs in your community?
8. Is your truancy rate increasing?
9. Are your suspension and expulsion rates increasing?
10. Have you had increased conflicts relative to dress styles, food services, and types of music played at special events?
11. Do you have an increasing number of students on probation in your school?
12. Have you had isolated racial fights?
13. Have you reduced the number of extracurricular programs and sports at your school?
14. Has there been an increasing incidence of parents withdrawing students from your school because of fear?
15. Has your budget for professional development opportunities and in-service training for your staff been reduced or eliminated?
16. Are you discovering more weapons on your campus?
17. Do you have written screening and selection guidelines for new teachers and other youth-serving professionals who work in your school?
18. Are drugs easily available in or around your school?
19. Are more than 40% of your students bused to school?
20. Have you had a student demonstration or other signs of unrest within the past 12 months?

Scoring and Interpretation

Multiply each *affirmative* answer by 5 and add the total.

   0-20 Indicates no significant school safety problems.

  25-45 An emerging school safety problem (safe school plan should be developed).

  50-70 Significant potential for school safety problem (safe school plan should be developed).

Over 70 School is a sitting time bomb (safe school plan should be developed immediately).

Reprinted with permission of the National School Safety Center, Ronald D. Stephens, Executive Director. Phone: (805) 373-9977. Website: www.nssc1.org

Appendix B

Oregon School Safety Survey

Developed by
Jeffrey Sprague, Geoffrey Colvin, & Larry Irvin
The Institute on Violence and Destructive Behavior
University of Oregon, College of Education

For further information contact Jeffrey Sprague, Ph.D., at 541-346-3592
jsprague@ccmail.uoregon.edu

Essential Questions for School Safety Planning

Please take a few minutes to complete the attached survey. Please place a check (X) next to the item that best reflects your opinion for each question. Your responses will be valuable in determining training and support needs related to school safety and violence prevention.

Your Role: Administrator __ Teacher __ Special Education Teacher __ Parent __
        Related Service Provider __ Community Member __ Student __ Other __

Your School: Elementary __ Middle/Junior High __ High School __ Alternative School __

Number of Students: Less than 500 __ 501-1000 __ More than 1000 __

Location: Rural __ Small Urban City __ (< 250,000) __ Large Urban City (> 250,000) __

Section One

Assessment of Risk Rating Factors for School Safety and Violence	Rating				
Indicate the extent to which these factors exist in your school and neighborhood:	Not at all	Minimally	Moderately	Extensively	Don't know
1. Illegal weapons					
2. Vandalism					
3. High student mobility (i.e. frequent changes in school enrollment)					
4. Graffiti					
5. Gang activity					
6. Truancy					
7. Student suspensions and/or expulsions					
8. Students adjudicated by the court					
9. Parents withdrawing students from school because of safety concerns					
10. Child abuse in the home					
11. Trespassing on school grounds					
12. Poverty					
13. Crimes (e.g. theft, extortion, hazing)					
14. Illegal drug and alcohol use					
15. Fights, conflict, and assault					
16. Incidence of bullying, intimidation, and harassment					
17. Deteriorating condition of the physical facilities in the school					

Section Two

Assessment of Response Plans for School Safety and Violence Rating	Rating				
Indicate the extent to which these factors exist in your school and neighborhood:	**Not at all**	**Minimally**	**Moderately**	**Extensively**	**Don't know**
18. Opportunity for extracurricular programs and sports activities.					
19. Professional development and staff training					
20. Crisis and emergency response plans					
21. Consistently implemented schoolwide discipline plans					
22. Student support services in school (e.g. counseling, monitoring, support team systems)					
23. Parent involvement in school (e.g. efforts to enhance school safety, student support)					
24. Student preparation for crises and emergencies					
25. Supervision of students across all settings					
26. Suicide prevention/response plans					
27. Student participation and involvement in academic activities					
28. Positive school climate for learning					
29. Acceptance of diversity.					
30. Response to conflict and problem solving					
31. Collaboration with community resources					
32. High expectations for student learning and productivity					
33. Effective student-teacher relationships					

Section Three

Your Comments on School Safety and Violence

1.   What is the most pressing safety need in your school?

2.   What school safety activities does your school do best?

3.   What topics are most important for training and staff development?

4.   What are the biggest barriers to improved school safety measures?

5.   What other comments do you have regarding school safety?

6.   What other factors not included in this survey do you believe affect school safety?

Bibliography

Anderson, Elijah. *Code of the Street: Decency, Violence, and the Moral Life of the Inner City.* New York: W. W. Norton, 1999.

Center on Juvenile and Criminal Justice/National Center on Institutions and Alternatives. *An Analysis of Juvenile Homicides.* Alexandria, Virginia, 1996. 14 pages.

Center to Prevent Handgun Violence. *Caught in the Crossfire: A Report on Gun Violence in our Nation's Schools,* 1990. 10 pages. ED 325 950.

Crowe, Timothy. "Designing Safer Schools." *Journal of School Safety* (Fall 1990): 9-13. EJ 419 891.

Curwin, Richard L., and Allen N. Mendler. *As Tough as Necessary: Countering Violence, Aggression, and Hostility in Our Schools.* Alexandria, Virginia: Association for Supervision and Curriculum Development, 1997. 162 pages. ED 413 410.

Environmental Building Supplies www.ecoHouse.com

Gottfredson, Denise C. "School-Based Crime Prevention." In *Preventing Crime: What Works, What Doesn't, What's Promising,* by Lawrence Sherman, Denise Gottfredson, Doris Mackenzie, John Eck, Peter Reuter, and Shawn Bushway. 5-1 to 5-74. College Park, Maryland: Department of Criminology and Criminal Justice, 1997. ED 423 321.

Gottfredson, G.D., and D.C. Gottfredson *Victimization in the Schools.* New York: Plenum, Inc., 1985.

Green, Mary W. *The Appropriate and Effective Use of Security Technologies in U.S. Schools, A Guide for Practical School Security Applications.* Washington D.C.: National Institute of Justice, U.S. Department of Justice, (September 1999). 129 pages. www.ojp.usdoj.gov/nij

Grossman, Dave. *On Killing: The Psychological Cost of Learning To Kill in War and Society.* Boston: Little, Brown & Co., 1996. 366 pages.

Jeffery, C. R. *CPTED: Past, Present and Future.* A position paper prepared for the International CPTED Association at the 4th Annual International CPTED Association Conference, Mississauga, Ontario, Canada, 1999.

_____. *Crime Prevention Through Environmental Design.* Beverly Hills, California: Sage, 1971. 290 pages.

Justice Policy Institute/Children's Law Center www.cjcj.org/schoolhousehype/

Kachur, S. Patrick; G.M. Stennies; K.E. Powell; W. Modzeleski; R. Stephens; R. Murphy; M. Kresnow; D. Sleet; and R. Lowry. "School Associated Violent Deaths in the United States, 1992-94." *Journal of the American Medical Association* 275, 22 (1996): 1729-33.

Kenworthy, Tom. "Columbine Changes Schools' Inner World." *USA Today* (April 14, 2000). 1A.

Kingery, Paul. Presentation at College of Education, University of Oregon, February 29, 2000.

Kipnis, Aaron R. *Angry Young Men: How Parents, Teachers, and Counselors Can Help Bad Boys Become Good Men.* San Francisco: Jossey-Bass, 1999. 277 pages.

Moos, Rudolph., and Paul Insel. *Issues in Social Ecology: Human Milieus.* Palo Alto, California: National Press Books, 1974. 616 pages.

National Association of Elementary School Principals. National Poll, 1997.

Newman, Oscar. *Defensible Spaces: Crime Prevention through Urban Design.* New York: MacMillan, 1972.

Noguera, Pedro A. "Preventing and Producing Violence: A Critical Analysis of Responses to School Violence." *Harvard Educational Review* 65, 2 (Summer 1995).: 189-212. EJ 504 542.

Norris, Clive, and Gary Armstrong. *The Maximum Surveillance Society; The Rise of CCTV.* Oxford, England: Berg Publishers, 1999. 248 pages.

Peart, K. N. "Lessons in Survival." *Scholastic Update* 126 (1994).

Plaster, Sherry, and Stan Carter. *Planning for Prevention: Sarasota, Florida's Approach to Crime Prevention through Environment Design.* Tallahassee, Florida: Florida Criminal Justice Executive Institute, Florida Department of Law Enforcement, 1993.

Richard, Alan. "NCES Report Pegs School Repair Costs at $127 Billion." *Education Week* XIX, 42 (July 12, 2000): 10.

Romer, D., and T. Heller. "Social Adaptation of Mentally Retarded Adults in Community Settings: A Social-Ecological Approach." *Applied Research in Mental Retardation* 4 (1983): 303-14.

Sabo, Sandra R. "Security by Design." *The American School Board Journal* 80, 1 (January 1993): 37-39. EJ 455 723.

Schalock, R. L. "Person-Environment Analysis: Short and Long-Term Perspectives. " In *Economics, Industry and the Disabled: A Look Ahead*, edited by W. E. Kiernan and R. L. Schalock. 115-127. Baltimore, Maryland: Paul H. Brookes, 1989.

Schalock, R. L., and C. M. Jensen. "Assessing the Goodness-of-Fit between Persons and their Environments." *The Journal of the Association for Persons with Severe Handicaps* 11, 2 (1986): 103-09.

Sprague, J.R., and H.M. Walker. "Early Identification and Intervention for Youth with Antisocial and Violent Behavior." In *Building Safe and Responsive Schools: Perspectives on School Discipline and School Violence*, edited by R. Skiba and R.L. Peterson, 2000.

Stover, D. "High Schools or High-Tech Prisons?" *Education Digest* 60 (1994).

"Teacher's Presence May Deter Violence."USA Today 125, 2619 (December 1996): 13.

Walker, H.M., and J. Eaton-Walker. "Key Questions about School Safety: Critical Issues and Recommended Solutions." *NASSP Bulletin* 84, 614 (March 2000): 46-55.

Wekerle, Gerda R., and Planning and Development Department Staff. *A Working Guide for Planning and Designing Safer Urban Environments.* Toronto: Safe City Committee of the City of Toronto, Canada, 1992.

Wekerle, Gerda R., and Carolyn Whitzman. *Safe Cities: Guidelines for Planning, Design, and Management.* Van Nostrand Reinhold, 1995.

Website Resources on School Safety

Trends and Issues

Discussion of School Safety and Violence Prevention
  The Scope of the Problem
  Cause for Concern
  Encouraging Signs
  Striving for Solutions
  Assess School-Based Characteristics
  Be Aware of Individual Risk Factors and Protective Factors
  Be Aware of Potential Underlying Influences
  Focus on Early and Ongoing Intervention
  Offer Social-Skills Training and Violence-Prevention Curricula
  Some Areas of Controversy
  Engage in Student "Profiling" and Other Techniques?
  Increase Building Security?
  Impose Stiffer Sentences on Juvenile Offenders?

Legislative Testimony by Dr. Hill Walker, codirector of the Institute on Violence and Destructive Behavior, College of Education, University of Oregon:

1. Key Questions About School Safety
2. Oregon Senate Bill 555—the importance of early identification of and intervention with children who may be at risk of antisocial behavior

ERIC Abstracts on School Safety

Violence Prevention Policy
Programs and Strategies
Bullying and Harassment
Gangs
Discipline Issues
Roots and Causes of Violence
Research on Violence

ERIC Digests on School Safety

ERIC Digest 134: Sexual Misconduct by School Employees
ERIC Digest 132: The Fundamentals of School Security
ERIC Digest 117: Student Dress Codes
ERIC Digest 94: School Violence Prevention

To view these and other full-text resources on a variety of topics related to educational policy and management, go to our award-winning website:

http://eric.uoregon.edu

Other Publications
Available from the ERIC Clearinghouse
on Educational Management

 Learning Experiences in School Renewal: An Exploration of Five Successful Programs
Bruce Joyce and Emily Calhoun • 1996 • 6 x 9 inches • viii + 208 pages • perfect bind • ISBN: 0-86552-133-6 • $14.50.
    Code: EMOLES

 Measuring Leadership: A Guide to Assessment for Development of School Executives
Larry Lashway • 1999 • 6x9 inches • viii + 117 pages • perfect bind
• ISBN 0-86552-140-9
•$9.75.Code: EMOMLG.

 Leading with Vision
Larry Lashway • 1997 • 6 x 9 inches • xii + 148 pages • perfect bind • ISBN: 0-86552-138-7 • $13.50. Code: EMOLWV

 Roadmap to Restructuring: Charting the Course of Change in American Education
David T. Conley • Second Edition • 1997 • 6 x 9 inches • xvi + 571 pages • Cloth ISBN: 0-86552-136-0 ($34.95) Code: EMORMC • Paper ISBN 0-86552-137-9 ($23.95) Code: EMORMP

 School Leadership: Handbook for Excellence
Edited by Stuart C. Smith and Philip K. Piele • Third Edition • 1997 • xvi + 432 pages • Cloth ISBN 0-86552-134-4 ($29.95) Code: EMOSLC • Paper ISBN 0-86552-135-2 ($19.95) Code: EMOSLP

 Student Motivation: Cultivating a Love of Learning
Linda Lumsden • 1999 • 6x9 inches • vi + 113 pages • perfect bind • ISBN 0-86552-141-7 •$9.50. Code: EMOSMC.

How to Order: You may place an order by sending a check or money order, mailing or faxing a purchase order, or calling with a Visa or MasterCard number. Add 10% for S&H (minimum $4.00). Make payment to University of Oregon/ERIC. Shipping is by UPS ground or equivalent.

Telephone (800) 438-8841

Fax (541) 346-2334

Publications Sales
ERIC Clearinghouse on Educational Management
5207 University of Oregon
Eugene, OR 97403-5207

You can also order online (with Visa or MasterCard) from our website—your gateway to information about educational policy and management.

http://eric.uoregon.edu